TOP 10 MILAN AND THE LAKES

REID BRAMBLETT

EYEWITNESS TRAVEL

Left **Villa Balbianello, Lake Como** Centre **Stazione Centrale, Milan** Right **Isola Bella: Borromeo Tombs**

LONDON, NEW YORK,
MELBOURNE, MUNICH AND DELHI
www.dk.com

Produced by Blue Island Publishing

Printed and bound in China by
Leo Paper Products Ltd

First published in the UK in 2003
by Dorling Kindersley Limited
80 Strand, London WC2R 0RL
A Penguin Company

13 14 15 16 10 9 8 7 6 5 4 3 2 1

Reprinted with revisions 2005, 2007, 2009, 2011, 2013

A CIP catalogue record is available from the British Library.

ISBN: 978-1-4093-7338-4

Within each Top 10 list in this book, no hierarchy of quality or popularity is implied. All 10 are, in the editor's opinion, of roughly equal merit.

MIX
Paper from responsible sources
FSC™ C018179

Contents

Milan and the Lakes Top 10

The information in this DK Eyewitness Top 10 Travel Guide is checked regularly.
Every effort has been made to ensure that this book is as up-to-date as possible at the time of going to press. Some details, however, such as telephone numbers, opening hours, prices, gallery hanging arrangements and travel information are liable to change. The publishers cannot accept responsibility for any consequences arising from the use of this book, nor for any material on third party websites, and cannot guarantee that any website address in this book will be a suitable source of travel information. We value the views and suggestions of our readers very highly. Please write to: Publisher, DK Eyewitness Travel Guides, Dorling Kindersley, 80 Strand, London, WC2R 0RL, UK, or email: travelguides@dk.com

Cover: Front – **SuperStock**: Jean Pierre Lescourret main. Back – **DK Images**: Paul Harris and Anne Heslope tc, tl, tr. Spine – **DK Images**: Paul Harris and Anne Heslope b.

Left **Lake Lugano vineyards** Centre **Rocca di Angera, Lake Maggiore** Right **Gelato shop**

Left **Galleria Vittorio Emanuele II, Milan** Right **Mantua**

Key to abbreviations
Adm *admission charge payable* **A/C** *air conditioning*

TOP 10 OF MILAN AND THE LAKES

TOP 10 Highlights of Milan and the Lakes

Milan is Italy's economic powerhouse, a bustling city of finance and industry, media empires and fashion houses, backed up by an impressive cultural heritage of important art galleries and ancient churches. Yet a 40-minute train ride takes you to the azure pools of "the lakes", lined with fishing villages, villas and laid-back resorts.

Lake Como

1 Leonardo's Last Supper

One of the largest and most ingenious works created by the ultimate Renaissance Man. It is in an advanced state of deterioration now, but even the shadow that remains of this great work can teach us volumes about Renaissance ideals *(see pp8–9)*.

2 Milan's Duomo

The world's largest Gothic cathedral took more than 400 years to complete, a forest of stone pinnacles, flying buttresses, more than 3,500 statues and fantastic panoramas from its roof *(see pp10–11)*.

3 Pinacoteca di Brera

Northern Italy's greatest painting gallery displays masterpieces by Mantegna, Giovanni Bellini, Piero della Francesca, Raphael and Caravaggio *(see pp12–15)*.

4 Castello Sforzesco

A sprawling 15th-century castle, now home to collections of tapestries, archaeological artifacts, paintings by Bellini and Mantegna, and sculptures that include Michelangelo's final work, the *Rondanini Pietà* *(see pp16–17)*.

Previous pages **Milan's Gothic Duomo**

5 Pinacoteca Ambrosiana

This cultural study centre founded in the 17th century contains works by Leonardo, Botticelli, Raphael and Caravaggio *(see pp18–19)*.

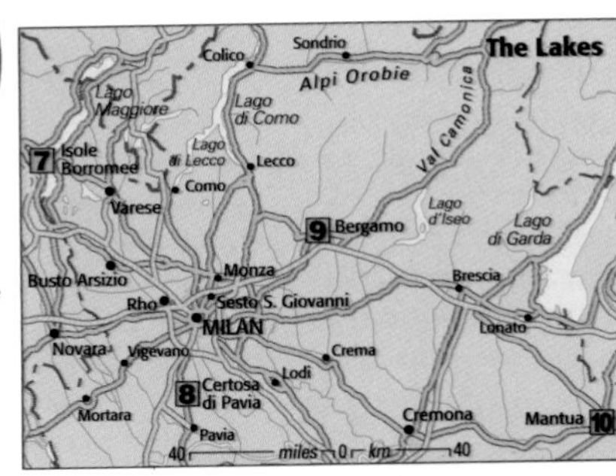

Sant'Ambrogio 6

One of the oldest churches in Milan, it was founded by the city's bishop and patron saint Ambrose in 379. It's filled with mosaics and carvings dating back to the 4th century *(see pp20–21)*.

7 Lake Maggiore's Isole Borromee

Three verdant islands, one still dominated by a fishing village, the other two clad in the sumptuous villas and ornate gardens of the local ruling Borromeo clan *(see pp22–3)*.

Certosa di Pavia 8

The pinnacle of the Lombard Renaissance, a vast monastery and church complex in the Po plains with an ornate marble façade, exquisite carved tombs, and some excellent paintings and frescoes *(see pp24–5)*.

9 Bergamo

The perfect balance of small town charm and sophisticated culture, medieval streets and Renaissance buildings, chic boutiques and hearty home-cooking *(pp26–7)*.

10 Mantua

The ancient seat of the Gonzaga dukes – ringed on three sides by shallow lakes – boasts Renaissance palaces designed and decorated by the likes of Mantegna and Giulio Romano *(see pp28–9)*.

TOP 10 Leonardo's Last Supper

The Last Supper, Leonardo da Vinci's 1495–7 masterpiece, is a touchstone of Renaissance painting. Since the day it was finished, art students have journeyed to Milan to view the work, which takes up a refectory wall in a Dominican convent next to the church of Santa Maria delle Grazie. The 20th-century writer Aldous Huxley called it "the saddest work of art in the world": he was referring not to the impact of the scene – the moment when Christ tells his disciples "one of you will betray me" – but to the fresco's state of deterioration.

Santa Maria delle Grazie

Book as far ahead as possible, especially if you are visiting during the holidays.

The informative audio guide will help explain why such a deteriorated fresco is nevertheless so important.

A few blocks down Via Magenta at via Carducci 13, Bar Magenta takes up a wide corner, a pleasing blend of Art Nouveau café and Guinness pub *(see p65).*

• Map J3 • Tourist info: Piazza S Maria delle Grazie 2/Corso Magenta, Milan • 02-9280-0360 • www.cenacolovinciano.org; www.vivaticket.it (tickets) • 8:15am–6:45pm Tue–Sun • €6.50 plus €1.50 booking fee; free for EU citizens under 18 or over 65; book well in advance

Top 10 Features

1. Groupings
2. "Halo" of Jesus
3. Judas
4. The Table
5. Perspective
6. Light
7. Reflections
8. Coats of Arms Above Painting
9. Crucifixion on Opposite Wall
10. Example of Ageing

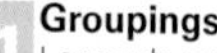

1 Groupings

Leonardo was at the time studying the effects of sound and physical waves. The groups of figures reflect the triangular Trinity concept (with Jesus at the centre) as well as the effect of a metaphysical shock wave, emanating out from Jesus and reflecting back from the walls as he reveals there is a traitor in their midst.

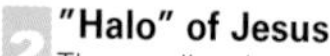

2 "Halo" of Jesus

The medieval taste for halos is satisfied without sacrificing Renaissance realism: Christ is set in front of a window *(below)*, giving him the requisite nimbus without looking as if he's wearing a plate for a hat.

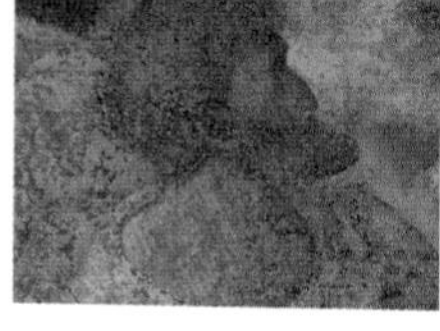

3 Judas

Previously Judas was often painted across the table from everyone else. Leonardo's approach is more subtle, and instead he places the traitor right among the other disciples *(above)*.

4 The Table

The table probably uses the same cloth and settings that the monks would have used, heightening the illusion that they were sharing their meals with Jesus and the Apostles.

For more on Leonardo da Vinci **see p48**

5 Perspective
The walls of the room in the painting appear to be continuations of the walls of the actual room you are standing in. The lines zoom in on Christ at the centre, drawing your eye towards his and helping to heighten the drama.

6 Light
Note the brilliant effects of the carefully worked interaction between the three sources of light – from the refectory itself, from the windows painted in the background, and from the windows on the refectory's left wall.

7 Reflections
A detail that heightens the illusion of reality: the colours of the disciples' robes are reflected in the glasses and pewter plates on the table *(above)*.

8 Coats of Arms Above Painting
The lunettes *(below)*, which are situated above the fresco, were also painted by Leonardo. It seems that he was as happy painting the perfect leaves around the Sforza coats of arms as he was composing the vast scene below.

9 Crucifixion on Opposite Wall
Most people spend so much time gazing at the *Last Supper* that they never notice the 1495 fresco by Donato Montorfano on the opposite wall, still rich with colour and vivid detail.

10 Example of Ageing
Montorfano's *Crucifixion* was painted in true *buon fresco*, but the now barely visible kneeling figures to the sides were added later on dry plaster – the same method Leonardo used.

A Vanishing Fresco

Rather than paint in *buon fresco* (the technique of applying pigment to wet plaster so that the colours bind with the base), Leonardo used oil paint on semi-dry plaster. Unfortunately, the image began to deteriorate even before he had finished the work.
To worsen matters, Napoleon's troops used the fresco for target practice, and bombs during World War II ripped off the building's roof. Restoration has removed centuries of over-painting by early "restorers" and filled in the completely vanished bits with pale washes.

TOP 10 Milan's Duomo

Milan's cathedral took almost 430 years to complete, from its 1386 inception to the façade's finishing touches in 1813 under Napoleon, but the builders stuck tenaciously to the Gothic style. In sheer figures it is impressive: it's the third largest church in the world, it has more than 3,500 exterior statues and is supported by 52 massive columns inside.

View of the roof

You cannot enter if your shoulders are bare or your shorts or skirt rise above mid-thigh; bring a light shawl or two.

On Milan's rare smog-free days, the view from the roof stretches across the plains as far as the Alps.

You're spoilt for café choice around here, but nothing beats a Campari at historic Zucca just inside the Galleria Vittorio Emanuele *(see pp64 & 80).*

- *Map M4*
- *Piazza del Duomo, Milan*
- *02-720-3375*
- *Cathedral: 7:30am–7:30pm daily, free*
- *Roof: 9am–6:30pm (to 4:45pm mid-Feb–mid-Nov) daily, €10 by elevator, €6 by stairs*
- *Museo del Duomo: Piazza del Duomo 14,*
- *www.duomomilano.it*

Top 10 Highlights

1. Façade
2. Naves
3. Battistero Paleocristiano
4. Stained-Glass Windows
5. Funerary Monument to Gian Giacomo Medici
6. St Bartholomew Flayed
7. Ambulatory and Crypt
8. Ascent to Roof
9. La Madonnina
10. Museo del Duomo

1 Façade

From the 16th century, various top architects submitted designs for the façade, but it wasn't until 1805–13 that the Neo-Gothic frontage with its bronze doors and reliefs *(above)* was finally built. The impressive central bronze door is by the Milanese sculptor, Ludovico Pogliaghi.

2 Naves

The interior *(right)* is a thicket of 52 pilasters ringed with statues of saints in niches. The Gothic "tracery" on the vaulting of the four outer naves is actually ingenious trompe l'oeil paintings dating from the 16th century. The gloom helps the illusion.

3 Battistero Paleocristiano

A stairway near the entrance leads down to Paleochristian excavations, which have uncovered traces of Roman baths from the 1st century BC, a baptistery from AD 287 and a 4th-century basilica.

The Duomo's façade before cleaning

For more marvellous churches in Lombardy **see pp38–9**

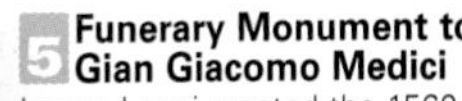

4 Stained-Glass Windows

Dozens of stained-glass windows *(left)* create splashes of coloured light in the otherwise gloomy interior. The oldest, on the right aisle, date from 1470; the newest from 1988.

5 Funerary Monument to Gian Giacomo Medici

Leone Leoni created the 1560–63 Michelangelesque tomb of a local mercenary general, including a life-sized bronze of the man dressed in Roman centurion armour.

Duomo plan

6 St Bartholomew Flayed

Marco d'Agrate's gruesome carving of 1562 shows the unfortunate saint with muscles and veins exposed and his flayed skin thrown rather jauntily over one shoulder.

7 Ambulatory and Crypt

The ambulatory is now open only to worshippers, but you can see a lovely example of a 14th-century Lombard sacristy door. Stairs nearby lead down into the crypt, where the body of Saint Charles Borromeo rests in a crystal coffin, and to the treasury, which is filled with elegant reliquaries and liturgical devices.

8 Ascent to Roof

Climb or take the lift up to the roof to explore the cathedral's remarkable Gothic crown of spires, gargoyles, statues and tracery *(above)* – and for the views *(see also p34)*.

9 La Madonnina

Perched at the top of the Duomo's central spire, 108 m (354 ft) above ground level, the gilded copper "Little Madonna" *(right)* has governed over Milan's best panorama since 1774. For centuries she reigned as the highest point in the city until the Pirelli Tower *(see p37)* stole her title.

10 Museo del Duomo

Reopened after extensive renovations, the museum contains stained-glass windows and tapestries removed from the Duomo for safekeeping. There is a masterpiece by Tintoretto, *The Infant Christ among the Doctors*, and wooden models of the Duomo.

La Fabbrica del Duomo

There's no better example of Milanese tenacity than the fact that their cathedral is a totally unspoilt example of the Gothic style, despite taking a full 427 years to build. The generations of builders somehow ignored the siren calls of every new style that came along, from Renaissance, then Baroque, to Neo-Classical. The phrase *la fabbrica del Duomo* – "the building of the Duomo" – in Milanese dialect is still used to refer to anything that seems to take forever to complete.

TOP 10 Pinacoteca di Brera

Milan's Brera is unique among Italy's major art galleries in that it isn't founded on the riches of the church or a noble family, but the policies of Napoleon, who suppressed churches across the region and took their riches off to galleries and academies. Over the next two centuries, the collections grew to take in some of the best Renaissance-era painting from northern Italy, representatives of the Venetian school and several giants of central Italy, including Raphael and Piero della Francesca.

Pinacoteca di Brera

Make sense of the works on display with the excellent audio guides.

Cheap guided tours for any number of people are available weekdays, but must be booked 2–3 days in advance.

The bars of the Brera district *(see p90)* make for great snacking or a post-gallery apéritif.

• Map M2 • Via Brera 28, Milan • 02-722-631; information line 02-8942-1146 • www.brera.beniculturali.it • 8:30am–7:15pm Tue–Sun (last adm 6:30pm) • Adm; free for EU citizens under 18 or over 65

Top 10 Works of Art

1. Riot in the Galleria
2. Valle Romita Polyptych
3. Dead Christ
4. Virgin and Child
5. Finding the Body of St Mark
6. Montefeltro Altarpiece
7. Marriage of the Virgin
8. Supper at Emmaus
9. Bacino di San Marco
10. The Kiss

2 Gentile Fabriano's Valle Romita Polyptych

The Brera worked hard to reconstitute this altarpiece of 1410. The five main panels came with Napoleon; the other four were tracked down and purchased later.

3 Mantegna's Dead Christ

Mantegna was one of the Renaissance's greatest perspective virtuosos, and this is his foreshortened masterpiece, painted in about 1500 *(below)*.

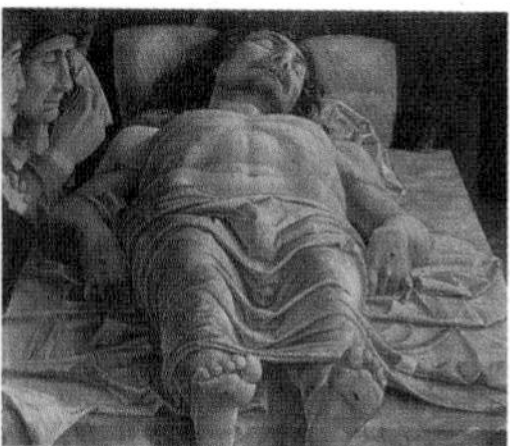

1 Umberto Boccioni's Riot in the Galleria

In this work of 1911 *(above)*, the Milanese are dashing for the doors of Caffè Zucca *(see p64)*. A companion, *The City Rises*, is also here.

Canaletto's *Bacino di San Marco*

4 Giovanni Bellini's Virgin and Child

The Brera houses several masterpieces by the early Venetian Renaissance master Bellini, including two very different versions of *Virgin and Child*. One is almost a Flemish-style portrait, painted when Bellini was 40. The other is a luminous scene of colour and light, painted 40 years later.

5 Tintoretto's Finding the Body of St Mark

Tintoretto uses his mastery of drama and light in this work of the 1560s to highlight the finding of the body of St Mark by Venetian merchants in the Crusades.

6 Piero della Francesca's Montefeltro Altarpiece

This 1472 scene shows Piero's patron the Duke of Montefeltro kneeling before the Virgin and Child. Just months earlier, the Duke's beloved wife had given birth to a male heir who tragically died within weeks.

Pinacoteca di Brera

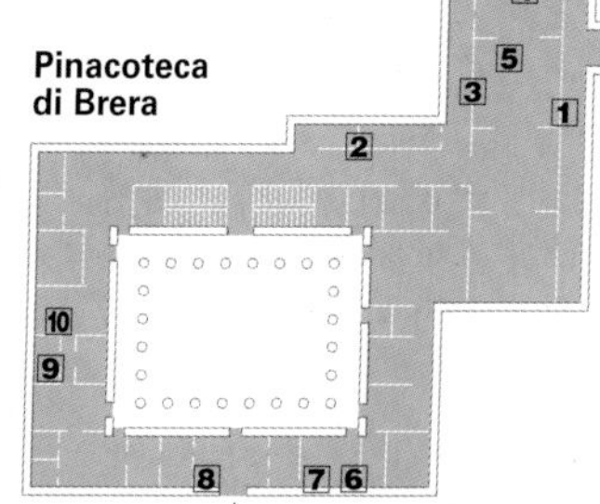

7 Raphael's Marriage of the Virgin

In this early work depicting the Virgin Mary's terrestrial marriage to Joseph, Raphael took the idea and basic layout from his Umbrian master Perugino, tweaking it with a perfected single-point perspective.

8 Caravaggio's Supper at Emmaus

This 1605 work *(above)* was Caravaggio's second painting of the Supper. The deep black shadows and bright highlights create mood and tension.

9 Canaletto's Bacino di San Marco

The undisputed master of 18th-century Venetian cityscapes did at least seven versions of this scene of St Mark's bell tower and the Doge's Palace *(above)*.

10 Francesco Hayez's The Kiss

This passionate 1859 scene *(left)* – painted when Hayez was 68 – was intended as an allegory of the struggle for independence and the importance of family.

The Palace

The late Baroque Palazzo di Brera was built from 1591 to 1658 as a Jesuit college, but not completed until 1774. The palace's vast courtyard centres around a bronze statue of Napoleon in the guise of Mars. The statue, commissioned in 1807, was installed 52 years later in 1859.

Brera gallery-goers

TOP 10 The Brera Collections

Titian's *Portrait of Count Antonio Porcia*

1 13th-Century Paintings (Rooms II–IV)

Italian art simply wouldn't be the same without the naturalism, bright colours and emotive qualities that Giotto brought to the world of painting, and his influence is clear in works such as *Three Scenes from the Life of St Columna* by Giovanni Baronzio of Rimini. Other works here trace the Gothic style from Central Italy (Ambrogio Lorenzetti and Andrea di Bartolo) to Venice (Lorenzo Veneziano and Jacopo Bellini). The best works are Ambrogio Lorenzetti's *Virgin and Child* and Gentile da Fabriano's *Valle Romita* polyptych.

2 Jesi Collection of 20th Century Art (Room X)

When Maria Jesi donated her fine hoard in 1976, the Brera became the first major museum in Italy to acquire a significant 20th-century collection. Boccioni's *Riot in the Galleria* is highlighted on p12; other masterworks are by Morandi, Severini, Modigliani, Picasso and Braque.

3 Venetian Renaissance (Rooms V-IX; XII; XIV)

It is the art of Venice that steals the show at the Brera, and the bulk of the museum's important and memorable works fill these ten rooms: Mantegna's *Dead Christ (see p12)* and numerous superlative works by his brother-in-law Giovanni Bellini. It all culminates in the brushy, stormy, wonderously lit and intriguingly coloured scenes of Venice's High Renaissance trio: Tintoretto, Titian and Paolo Veronese.

4 Lombard Renaissance (Rooms XIII; XV-XIX)

The stars of the Lombard section are the 16th-century Campi clan from Cremona, painters inspired by Raphael and, above all, Leonardo da Vinci. Tiny room XIX is devoted to the direct heirs of the Leonardo revolution: Il Bergognone and Bernardino Luini.

Valle Romita polyptych

5 Marchese Renaissance (Rooms XXI; XXIII)

These rooms feature Flemish-inspired artists and 15th-century

Raphael's *The Marriage of the Virgin*

painters from the central Marches province. The latter took local art from the post-Giotto Gothicism into a courtly Early Renaissance style, exemplified by Carlo Crivelli.

6 Tuscan Renaissance (Rooms XXIV–XXVII)

The paintings here are few, but they're stunners: Piero's *Montefeltro Altarpiece* and Raphael's *Marriage of the Virgin (both on p13)*, alongside works by Bramante, Signorelli and Bronzino.

7 17th-Century Bolognese Renaissance (Room XXVIII)

As Florence and Rome got swept away with Mannerist fantasies and experiments, Bolognese artists held the line on Classical Renaissance ideals. In this room we see Ludovico Caracci, Il Guercino and Guido Reni engaged in an ever more crystalline and reductive naturalistic style.

8 Caravaggio and his Followers (Room XXIX)

Caravaggio's use of harsh contrast and dramatic tension in paintings such as the *Supper at Emmaus (p13)* influenced a generation of painters. The works of some of the best of them – Mattia Preti,

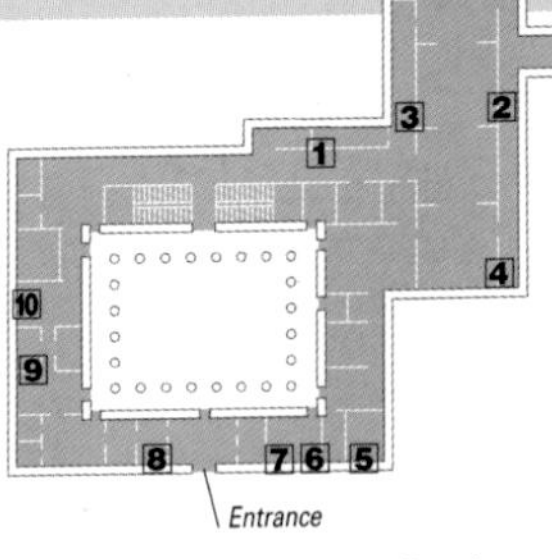

Jusepe de Ribera and Orazio Gentilleschi – are hung here too.

9 Baroque and Rococo (Rooms XXX–XXXVI)

In the late 16th century, Italy moved from Renaissance naturalism to the ever more ornate stylings of the Baroque, with Daniele Crespi and Pietro da Cortona to the fore. The Baroque fed off its own overblown conventions until it became Rococo, a style heralded by Tiepolo and Giuseppe Maria Crespi.

10 19th-Century Painting (Rooms XXXVII–XXXVIII)

There's not so much to pique one's interest in these final rooms, save Francesco Hayez's monumental scenes and the pseudo-Impressionist Macchiaioli school (Fattori, Segantini and Lega).

Modigliani's *Portrait of Moise Kisling*

TOP 10 Castello Sforzesco

This massive, sun-baked rectangular bastion in Milan is actually a complex of fortresses, castles and towers begun in 1451 for Francesco Sforza, largely restored in 1893–1904, and again after massive World War II damage. Its many collections include art and sculpture from the early Middle Ages to the 18th century, decorative arts, musical instruments, Oriental art, and archaeology.

Madonna in Glory by Mantegna

Main gate

Ask about special tours that can get you into many non-museum sections of the castle that are normally closed to the public.

The snack vans on-site are over-priced, and the nearest bars are best avoided. Head down Via Dante to the café at no. 15, where you can enjoy panini and *gelato*.

* *Map K2 • Piazza Castello, Milan; 02-8846-3700; www.milanocastello.it; 9am–7pm daily (6pm winter); free*
* *Musei Civici: 02-8846-3703; 9am–5:30pm Tue–Sun; adm €3 (free from 2pm Fri)*

Top 10 Highlights

1. Rondanini Pietà
2. Funerary Monument for Gaston de Foix
3. Sala delle Asse
4. Madonna in Glory
5. Madonna and Child
6. Poet Laureate
7. Lorenzo Lenzi
8. Trivulzio Tapestries
9. Cappella Ducale
10. Parco Sempione

1 Michelangelo's Rondanini Pietà

Michelangelo started his career with a *Pietà* carved at the age of 25 (now in St Peter's, Rome), and while the master was famous for not finishing his statues, in this instance it was not his fault. At the age of 89, in 1564, he was struck down (probably by a stroke) literally while chipping away at this sculpture *(below, right)*.

2 Funerary Monument for Gaston de Foix

Gaston de Foix was Duke of Nemours, Marshall of France, ruler of the French Milan Duchy, post-humous hero of the 1512 Battle of Ravenna and Louis XII's nephew. His tomb's ethereally sculpted elements, carved by Bambaia in 1510, are now dispersed *(see box)*.

One of the *Trivulzio Tapestries* (the month of September)

3 Sala delle Asse

The "Plank Hall" was decorated in 1498 by Leonardo da Vinci with a trompe l'oeil arbour of geometrically intricate vines on the vaulted ceiling. This was painted over many times; the only bit we can be sure is original is a mono-chrome sketch of a twisting root, on the wall between the two windows.

4 Mantegna's Madonna in Glory

Bellini's famous brother-in-law painted this magnificent altarpiece *(left)* for a Verona church in 1497, making it one of his final works. The harshness of his youthful style is tempered by age and experience to yield this solid, naturalistic approach.

5 Bellini's Madonna and Child

This is an early Bellini *(above)*, painted 1468–70, with touching detail. Mary wears a pearl-trimmed pink shawl. Jesus gazes at a lemon in his hand.

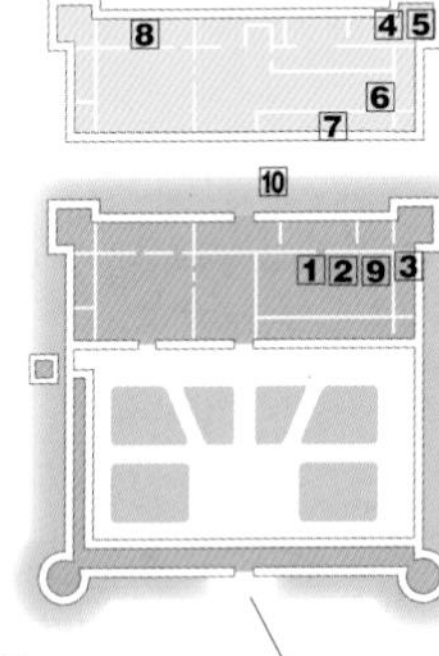

Entrance

Key

Ground floor

First floor

6 Bellini's Poet Laureate

The attribution of this portrait *(below)*, painted in 1475, has wavered between Bellini and Antonella da Messina. There is an almost Flemish attention to detail in the hair and eyes of the subject.

8 Trivulzio Tapestries

The *Tapestries of the Twelve Months (above)* were designed by Bramantino in 1503 and named for the man who commissioned them, General Gian Giacomo Trivulzio.

9 Cappella Ducale

The Ducal chapel has the original frescoes painted in 1472 by Stefano de Fedeli and Bonifacio Bembo for Galeazzo Maria Sforza, including a *Resurrection* and an *Annunciation.*

7 Bronzino's Lorenzo Lenzi

A Mannerist painter at the Medici court in Florence, Bronzino's delicate portrait shows a sensitivity to his subject's youthful restlessness.

10 Parco Sempione

The 47-hectare (115-acre) park northwest of the castle is central Milan's largest green space. A public park since 1893, many of its structures are fine early 20th-century Art Nouveau *(see p85).*

Gaston de Foix's Tomb

In 1510, King Francis I ordered a tomb for the young hero. Bambaia executed an effigy of the warrior lying in state and beautiful high relief panels. When the French pulled out of Milanese affairs in 1522, the tomb was unfinished. The pieces were sold off, winding up here, in the Ambrosiana *(see p19)*, in Turin and in London.

TOP 10 Pinacoteca Ambrosiana

Local Cardinal Frederico Borromeo founded this library (of some 36,000 manuscripts and over 750,000 prints) and painting gallery in Milan in 1603 after a formative time spent in Rome's artistic circles. It was (and is) a place in which to study theological issues via academic tomes and works of art, a truly Renaissance mix of religion, intellectualism and aesthetics. There are paintings by such greats as Tiepolo, Francesco Hayez and Jan Brueghel.

The courtyard

Just around the corner from the gallery, on Via Spadari, you will find Peck *(see p68)*, one of Italy's best food emporia and oversized *tavole calde* (bars).

- *Map L4*
- *Piazza Pio XI 2*
- *02-806-921*
- *www.ambrosiana.it*
- *10am–6pm (last adm 5:30pm) Tue–Sun*
- *Adm €15, concessions €10*

Top 10 Works of Art

1. Madonna del Padiglione
2. Portrait of a Musician
3. Codex Atlantico
4. Adoration of the Magi
5. Holy Family
6. Rest on the Flight into Egypt
7. Cartoon for School of Athens
8. Basket of Fruit
9. Landscape with St Paul
10. Detail from the Tomb of Gaston de Foix

Page from *Codex Atlantico*

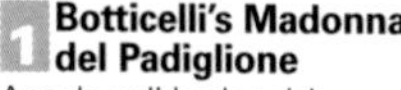

1 Botticelli's Madonna del Padiglione

Angels pull back a rich canopy to reveal a scene of Mary and Jesus in a pastoral setting *(below left)*. This work dates from the 1490s, after Botticelli's religious crisis turned him from the famed mythological scenes of his brilliant youth.

2 Leonardo's Portrait of a Musician

This portrait *(right)*, quasi-Flemish in pose and detail, yet glowing with a sense of human psychology typical of Leonardo, has been said to be of various subjects, but most likely depicts a musician of the Sforza court. It is almost certainly by Leonardo, but probably retouched over the years.

3 Leonardo's Codex Atlantico

Reproductions of pages from these oversized tomes *(above)* reside inside glass-topped tables. They are filled with Leonardo da Vinci's sketches.

4 Titian's Adoration of the Magi

This courtly tumble of the three kings kissing the toes of baby Jesus in his manger was part of Frederico Borromeo's original collection, a complex work from 1560 that the cardinal described as "a school for painters".

5 Luini's Holy Family

If this looks familiar, it is because, especially early on, Luini was almost slavishly devoted to the manner of his master Leonardo da Vinci, and in fact this painting is based on a famous drawing by Leonardo.

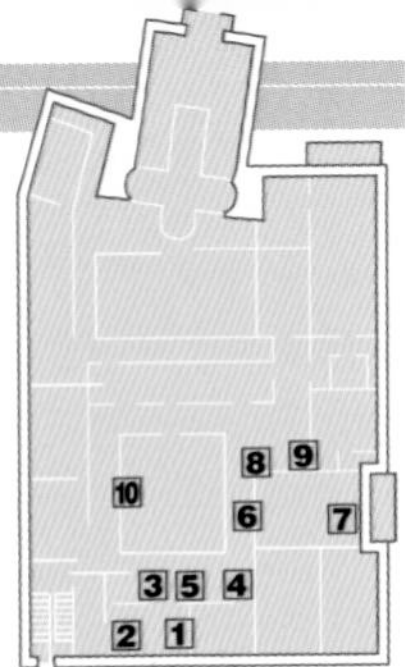

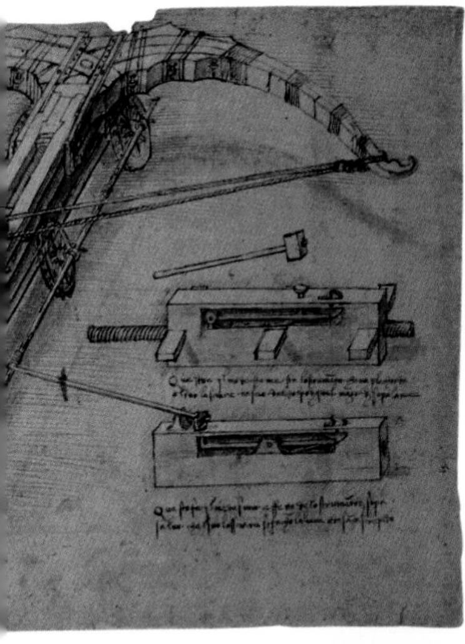

6 Bassano's Rest on the Flight into Egypt

The Venetian master Jacopo Bassano was turning to a densely coloured palette, rich in contrasting tones, when he produced this work *(below)* in 1547.

7 Raphael's Cartoon for School of Athens

This is the preparatory drawing for Raphael's famous fresco of Greek philosophers with the faces of Renaissance artists *(below)*.

8 Caravaggio's Basket of Fruit

This still life was probably acquired from Caravaggio by the cardinal during his Roman sojourn. The painting shows how Caravaggio was, even at the age of 25, perfecting the hyper-realism he would soon apply to large canvases and more complex scenes.

9 Bril's Landscape with St Paul

This is the most dramatic of the over half-dozen Bril works on display, showcasing how Bril managed to work with the early 17th-century's most popular sacred scenes but set them in his beloved, intricately executed landscape form.

10 Bambaia's Detail from the Tomb of Gaston de Foix

The Milanese sculptor Bambaia carved this series of small marble panels with delicate figures surrounded by military accoutrements and mythological creatures, all in extraordinary high relief. This is but a part of the work; most of the monument is in the Castello Sforzesco *(see pp16–17)*.

Raphael's Revelation

In the final *School of Athens* fresco, Michelangelo (depicted as Heraclitus) lounges on the central steps. The detail is missing in this sketch because Raphael only added him when, half-way through painting, he got a glimpse of the Sistine Chapel and was deeply impressed.

TOP 10 Sant'Ambrogio

One of Milan's oldest basilicas (founded by St Ambrose in 379) served as a model for most of the city's early medieval churches. It was enlarged in the 9th century, and what we see today dates largely from 1080 (albeit with later reconstructions). It instantly became Milan's most beloved house of worship when the wildly popular (and future patron saint) Ambrose was buried here in 397. Everything is well signposted in Italian and English.

Nave

The best of the more portable objects formerly in the church treasury and small museum are now displayed in the Museo Diocesano *(see p93)*.

Walk northwest to the fabulous Art Nouveau café/pub Bar Magenta at Via Carducci 13 *(see p65)*.

• Map K4 • Piazza Sant'Ambrogio 15, Milan; 02-8645-0895; 7am–noon, 3–7pm daily; free
• San Vittore in Ciel d'Oro: 10am–noon, 3–5pm daily
• Museo della Basilica: 10am–noon, 2:30–6pm Tue–Sat, 3–6pm Sun; adm €2. No visitor access during Mass

Top 10 Highlights

1. Atrium
2. Façade
3. Serpent Column
4. Bergognone's Redeemer
5. Sarcophagus of Stilicho
6. Pulpit
7. Golden Altar
8. Ciborium
9. Apse Mosaics
10. Sacello di San Vittore in Ciel d'Oro

1 Atrium

The first clue that this church is something apart is the lovely, elongated atrium *(below)* between the entrance and the church, built from 1088 to 1099 using columns with 6th-century capitals depicting fantastical scenes.

2 Façade

The austere but balanced façade *(right)* consists of five arches fitted under the peaked roof line. It is flanked by two mismatched towers: the Monks' Tower on the right from the 9th century and the Canons' Tower on the left from 1144.

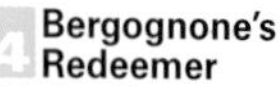

4 Bergognone's Redeemer

This limpid, late 15th-century Renaissance scene of the Risen Christ was originally positioned on the wall to the right of the altar (where its painted trompe l'oeil architecture was far more suited). It was later removed and placed in the first chapel on the left.

Golden altar

3 Serpent Column

Just on the inside of the third pier on the left stands a short column topped by a curlicue of a bronze serpent, a 10th-century Byzantine work (although local legend says it's the serpent cast by Moses).

6 Pulpit

This composite of 11th- and early 12th-century Romanesque relief panels was rescued after the church ceiling collapsed in 1196 and reconstructed into this magnificent pulpit *(left)*.

5 Sarcophagus of Stilicho

This late Roman-era sarcophagus *(above)* preceded the pulpit (No. 6) built around it. The tomb is aligned with the original walls, while the pulpit is aligned with the nave.

7 Golden Altar

A master goldsmith, Volvinio, crafted the "golden altar" in 835 *(below)*. The Life of Christ is in gold leaf on the front, and the Life of St Ambrose in gilded silver on the back.

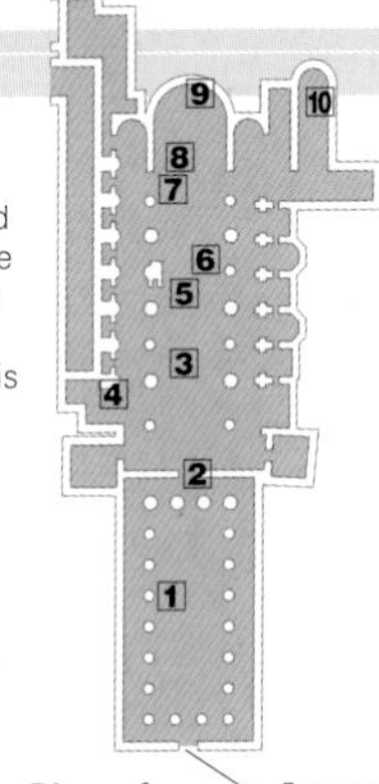

Plan of Basilica

8 Ciborium

This altar canopy *(below)* sits at the centre of the presbytery. Its four ancient Roman columns support a canopy of four 10th-century Lombard polychrome stucco reliefs.

9 Apse Mosaics

The vast, colourful mosaic depicting Christ Pantocrater *(above)* was largely pieced together between the 4th and 8th centuries, though bits were touched up or redone between the 17th and 20th centuries, especially after a 1943 bombing tore away half of Christ and the Archangel on the left.

10 Sacello di San Vittore in Ciel d'Oro

Sant'Ambrogio was built next to a Paleochristian cemetery and a chapel decorated in the 5th century with a glittering dome of almost solid gold mosaics. The basilica grew to include the chapel and its ancient mosaics.

St Ambrose

Ambrose (340–97) became Archbishop of Milan in 374, where he set about building the four great basilicas (this church, San Lorenzo, San Nazaro and San Simpliciano), tutoring St Augustine (whom he baptized into Christianity), and generally controlling the city from his bishop's throne. He was canonized soon after his death and became the city's patron.

Lake Maggiore's Isole Borromee

This trio of islets – Isola Bella ("Beautiful Island"), Isola Madre ("Mother Island") and Isola Superiore, or Isola dei Pescatori ("Isle of the Fishermen") – has been shaped by the Borromeo family, who in the 16th and 17th centuries turned Bella and Madre into vast garden-and-palace complexes. If you've time only for one, make it Isola Bella, though its ornate, formal gardens are less relaxing and botanically interesting than Isola Madre's.

Isola Madre gardens

Buy discounted island admission tickets along with your ferry ticket at the Stresa docks.

Isola Bella's gardens remain open all day, but access is via the Palazzo so you can't enter between noon and 1:30pm.

There are many cafés on Isola Bella's quay. Café Lago serves sandwiches, coffee and lager to a backdrop of rock music.

- *Map A2*
- *Access is from the ferry docks at Stresa* *(see p99)*
- *www.borromeoturismo.it*
- *Isola Bella: 0323-30-556; 22 Mar–26 Oct: 9am–5:30pm (Oct until 5pm) daily; adm €13, under-16s €5.50*
- *Isola Madre: 0323-31-261; 22 Mar–26 Oct: 9am–5:30pm (Oct until 5pm) daily; adm €11, under-16s €5.50*

Top 10 Highlights

1. Isola Bella: Borromeo Palace
2. Isola Bella: Sala di Musica in the Palace
3. Isola Bella: Tapestries in the Palace
4. Isola Bella: Grottoes
5. Isola Bella: Borromeo Tombs
6. Isola Bella: Gardens
7. Isola Madre: Villa Borromeo
8. Isola Madre: Botanical Gardens
9. Isola Madre: Kashmir Cypress
10. Isola Superiore

1 Isola Bella: Borromeo Palace

The vast Borromeo Palace and its grounds *(below)* dominate the island. The palace is largely 17th century, but wasn't finished until 1959. The sumptuous rooms have stucco ceilings and are filled with inlaid dressers, Murano chandeliers and fine paintings.

4 Isola Bella: Grottoes

Artificial caves were all the rage in the 18th century *(above)*. They were decorated with a sort of grand, intricate pebble-dash in black-and-white patterns.

Isola Bella Gardens

2 Isola Bella: Sala di Musica in the Palace

The palace's most important room is named for its collection of antique instruments. On 11 April 1935, Mussolini met here with Laval of France and Ramsay MacDonald of Britain in an attempt to stave off World War II.

3 Isola Bella: Tapestries in the Palace

This detail-rich series of 16th-century Flemish works is based on that popular theme for medieval tapestries: the unicorn (which is also a Borromeo heraldic totem).

5 Isola Bella: Borromeo Tombs

The "Private Chapel" was built in 1842–4 as a mausoleum for a pair of late Gothic/early Renaissance 15th-century family tombs as well as the 1522 Monument to the Birago Brothers, carved by Renaissance master Bambaia.

6 Isola Bella: Gardens

This pyramid of terraces *(left)* is topped by a unicorn, the edges lined by statue-laden balustrades. A few pairs of white peacocks strut over the clipped lawns.

7 Isola Madre: Villa Borromeo

This summer villa was built largely between 1518 and 1585. Today it is a museum with mannequins in Borromeo livery and paraphernalia from puppet theatres.

8 Isola Madre: Botanical Gardens

The surprisingly lush and extensive gardens *(above)* around the Villa Borromeo are filled with exotic flora. Take the time to walk around the island, past the azaleas, rhododendrons and camellias famous since the 19th century.

9 Isola Madre: Kashmir Cypress

Europe's largest cypress spreads its 200-year-old, weeping Oriental strands of needles over a gravel courtyard to one side of the Villa Borromeo.

10 Isola Superiore

The Borromei pretty much left this island (also known as Isola dei Pescatori, *right*) alone when they were converting its neighbours into sumptuous garden-palaces, allowing the island's fishing hamlet to develop more naturally into a tourist draw today.

The Borromeo Family

The Borromeo clan fled political intrigue in Tuscany for Milan in 1395, where they bankrolled the rise of the Visconti. Building a pan-European financial empire, they bought the Arona fiefdom in 1447 They skilfully tacked through the era's turbulent political winds, married wisely, and associated with the Sforza while slowly acquiring control of Lake Maggiore. The family still owns the islands.

For a day's itinerary including Isole Borromee **see p101**

TOP 10 Certosa di Pavia

Gian Galeazzo Visconti founded this charterhouse in 1396 as a vast family mausoleum, set 8 km (5 miles) north of Pavia. Finished in the mid-16th century under the Sforzas, it became one of the great monuments of the Lombard Renaissance. After the 1782 suppression of the Carthusian order, it was abandoned, then inhabited for brief spells until, in 1968, the Cistercians moved in to stay.

Façade of charterhouse

Avoid visiting at the weekend, when the sight is very crowded.

To get past the elaborate 1660 iron screen at the end of the nave, wait until one of the monks escorts a small group in to see the famous tombs and cloisters.

There's nowhere to eat near the Certosa, so either head into Pavia itself, or bring a picnic and buy some of the monks' liqueur.

• Map C5 • Via del Monumento 4, Pavia • 9–11am Tue–Sun; and Apr & Sep 2:30–5:30pm; May–Aug: 2:30–6pm; Oct & Mar: 2:30–5pm; Nov–Feb: 2:30–4:30pm • Free • For more details, contact Pavia's tourist office: 0382-59-7001

Top 10 Highlights

1. Façade
2. Perugino's Altarpiece
3. Bergognone's Works
4. St Ambrose with Saints
5. Funerary Monument of Ludovico il Moro and Beatrice d'Este
6. Ivory Altar
7. Tomb of Gian Galeazzo Visconti
8. Great Cloister
9. Little Cloister
10. Monks' Shop

1 Façade

The astounding and rich façade *(above left)* has decorative flourishes and polychrome marbles that set it apart and make it one of Italy's most important and idiosyncratic examples of late 15th-century architecture. The initial work was undertaken in 1473–99; the top part was continued after 1525, but never finished.

2 Perugino's Altarpiece

The central panel *(left)* of the *Eternal Father* (1499) is all that remains here of the original full altarpiece by Umbrian master (and Raphael's first teacher) Perugino. The flanking panels are by Bergognone, while below are 16th-century reproductions of the other, original Perugino panels.

The Little Cloister

3 Bergognone's Works

Bergognone rules the Certosa, providing altarpieces for three chapels, plus part of Perugino's altarpiece. He also frescoed the seventh chapel on the right *(detail, above)* and the ends of both transepts, brilliantly blue with lapis lazuli.

4 St Ambrose with Saints

In Bergognone's 1492 altarpiece in the sixth chapel on the left, St Ambrose is enthroned and surrounded by four saints. The group is in a setting similar to the chapel interior, to create the illusion that they are present.

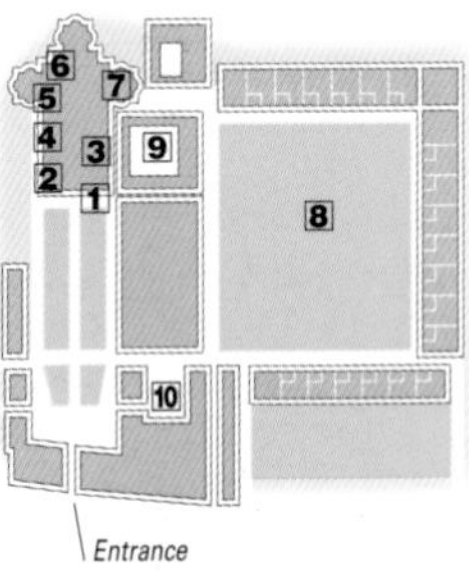

5 Funerary Monument of Ludovico il Moro and Beatrice d'Este

The most renowned work in the Certosa is an empty tomb *(see box)*, with remarkably lifelike effigies of the couple *(above, right)* lying in state, carved in 1497 by Cristoforo Solari.

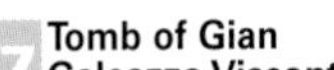

7 Tomb of Gian Galeazzo Visconti

It's only fitting that the Certosa's founder should be buried here, in a monument of 1492–7 depicting scenes from Visconti's life, carved by Gian Cristoforo Romano. The sarcophagus below is by Andrea Alessi, while the statues of the *Virgin*, *Fame* and *Victory* were added in the mid-16th century.

6 Ivory Altar

The Florentine sculptor Baldassare degli Embriachi carved this ivory triptych altarpiece (1400–1409), with 76 compartments and more than 100 tiny statues. It was stolen in 1984, leading to the uncovering of a ring of international art thieves outside Naples. The treasure, slightly damaged, was recovered.

8 Great Cloister

This large arcaded cloister *(below)* is lined with the homes of the Cistercian monks who still inhabit the Certosa. These are cosy little two-storey houses with a tiny private chapel and walled gardens at the back.

9 Little Cloister

Guiniforte Solari designed this lovely arcaded space for the monks to gather and contemplate – and probably admire the magnificent flank of the church above.

10 Monks' Shop

The Cistercian monks make their own Chartreuse liqueurs, herbal soaps and scents, which they sell here to the public.

A Peripatetic Tomb

The sad story behind the beautiful tomb of Ludovico il Moro and his wife Beatrice d'Este illustrates that even the best-laid plans of the mightiest men can go terribly awry. The duke and his wife were meant to be buried together in Milan's Santa Maria delle Grazie (where the *Last Supper* had just been painted). But Ludovico ended up dying in exile in France, so only Beatrice was buried in Milan, and the church, strapped for cash, sold the funerary monument to the Certosa in 1564.

For more on Pavia town **see p46**

Top 10 Bergamo

One of Northern Italy's surprising gems, Bergamo mixes medieval charm with a cultural sophistication that has made it popular among Italy's cognoscenti. Bergamo has been a split-level town since Roman times, when a civitas *(today's medieval Upper Town) perched atop the hill and a* suburbia *(the modernized Lower Town) spread into the plain.*

Baptistry

To get to the Upper Town from the train station, take bus 1 or 1A and transfer (free) to the Funicolare Bergamo Alta.

The Caffè della Funiculare has sweeping views over the valley ***(see also pp128–9.)***

- *Map D3*
- *Tourist info: IAT, www.comune.bergamo.it; Piazzale Papa Giovanni XXIII, 51 (Lower Town), 035-210-204; Viale Gombito 13 (Upper Town), 035-242-226*
- *Basilica: 9am–12:30pm (until 12:45pm Sun), 2:30–5pm daily (to 6pm Sat & Sun); free*
- *Museo Donizettiano: 9:30am–1pm, 2–5:30pm Tue–Sun; Oct–Mar: closed weekday pm; adm €5*
- *Castello di San Vigilio: 9am–dusk daily; free*
- *Galleria d'Arte: 10am–1pm, 3–7pm Tue–Sun*
- *Galleria dell'Accademia Carrara: Closed until at least 2013 for restoration*
- *Museo del 500 Veneto: 9:30am–1pm, 2:30–6pm; Tue–Sun (open all day Sat); adm €5*

Top 10 Sights

1. Piazza del Duomo
2. Piazza Vecchia
3. Cappella Colleoni
4. Basilica di Santa Maria Maggiore
5. Museo Donizettiano
6. Via Colleoni
7. Castello di San Vigilio
8. Galleria d'Arte Moderna e Contemporanea
9. Galleria dell'Accademia Carrara
10. Museo del 500 Veneto

Piazza Vecchia

1 Piazza del Duomo

This square is dominated by elaborate Bergamasco architecture: the entrance to Santa Maria Maggiore, the façade of the Capella Colleoni and a fanciful baptistery *(above left)* of 1340.

2 Piazza Vecchia

One of Northern Italy's most theatrical squares *(above right)* is surrounded by retro-medieval stone buildings, Renaissance palaces, a 12th-century tower and several historic cafés.

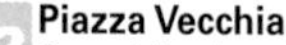

3 Cappella Colleoni

The anchor of the twinned Piazza Vecchia and Piazza del Duomo is this magnificent Renaissance chapel *(left)* devoted to Bergamo's warrior-lord Bartolomeo Colleoni. In pink and white patterned marble, it is covered with reliefs and Rococo frescoes.

4 Basilica di Santa Maria Maggiore

Inside the basilica *(left)*, every inch of ceiling is covered with frescoes. Against the back wall is the tomb of composer Gaetano Donizetti. The gorgeous, early 16th-century, inlaid wood panels fronting the choir are by Lorenzo Lotto.

5 Museo Donizettiano

Here are the original sheet music, piano *(left)* and memorabilia of Bergamo's early 19th-century composer Gaetano Donizetti. He died, in the very bed on display here, of syphilis in 1848.

6 Via Colleoni

The main drag of Bergamo's Upper Town is lined with shops and wine bars, modest medieval palaces and churches, tiny squares and half-timbered houses. It's closed to most traffic, and filled every evening with hordes of locals and visitors.

7 Castello di San Vigilio

Built by the town's Venetian lords in the 16th and 17th centuries, the castle in the hamlet of San Vigilio has been reduced to the romantic ruins you can see today, with a public garden boasting fine views.

8 Galleria d'Arte Moderna e Contemporanea

Bergamo's modern art gallery features exhibitions alongside a permanent collection with works by some of Italy's key 20th-century painters including Giovanni Fattori, Boccioni, De Chirico and Morandi.

9 Galleria dell' Accademia Carrara

During restoration, changing exhibits from this collection are on show at Palazzo della Ragione *(see p73)* in Piazza Vecchia, which includes works by Raphael, Botticelli *(above)* and Bellini.

10 Museo del 500 Veneto

Opened in 2012, this museum in the Palazzo Podesta explores life in the 16th century, taking the visitor on a journey from Venice to Bergamo through a series of interactive exhibits.

The Lower Town

Few visitors make it to the open, spacious streets of the Lower Town, laid out largely in the 20th century (but settled since Roman times). The chief boulevard of this vibrant area is the Sentierone ("big path"). This is where most Bergamaschi head of an evening to shop in the stores and meet at the cafés.

Mantua

This town is known for its fine palaces, its masterpieces by Mantegna and Giulio Romano and its position surrounded on three sides by wide, shallow, swamp-edged lakes. These man-made lakes make the area humid in summer and rather damp and chilly in winter, creating a slight air of melancholy. The poet Virgil was born here in 70 BC. By 1328, the town had come under the rule of the Gonzagas, who held onto the reigns of power until the Austrians took over in 1707.

Fresco in the Chamber of the Wind, Palazzo Te

Hire a bicycle from La Rigola, on Lungolago dei Gonzaga.

Caffè Miró is on the tiny piazza in front of Sant'Andrea. ***(see also pp128–9)***

• Map H6 • Tourist info: Piazza Mantegna 6 • 0376-432-432 • www.turismo.mantova.it • Duomo: 7am–noon, 3–7pm daily; free • Palazzo Ducale: 8:30am–7pm Tue–Sun; adm €6.50 • Sant'Andrea: 8am–noon, 3–7pm Mon–Fri; 10:30am–noon, 3–6pm Sat; 11:45am–12:15pm, 3–6pm Sun; free • Rotonda: 10am–1pm, 3–6pm Mon–Fri, 10am–6pm Sat & Sun; donation • Teatro Bibiena: 9:30am–12:30pm, 3–6pm Tue–Sun; adm €2 • Palazzo d'Arco: 10am–1pm, 3–6pm Tue–Fri; 9:30am–1pm, 2:30–6pm Sat & Sun (winter hours vary); adm €5 • Casa del Mantegna: 10am–12:30pm, 3–6pm Tue–Fri, 10am–6pm Sat & Sun; free • Palazzo Te: 9am–6pm Tue–Sun, 1–6pm Mon; adm €8

Top 10 Sights

1. Duomo
2. Palazzo Ducale
3. Piazza Broletto
4. Piazza delle Erbe
5. Basilica di Sant'Andrea
6. Rotunda di San Lorenzo
7. Teatro Scientifico Bibena
8. Palazzo d'Arco
9. Casa del Mantegna
10. Palazzo Te

1 Duomo

Fire claimed the Gothic cathedral. The façade *(right)* is late Baroque (1756–61), and Giulio Romano's interior was designed in imitation of Paleochristian basilicas.

2 Palazzo Ducale

Highlights in the Gonzagas' rambling fortress-palace *(above)* include tapestries by Raphael and Mantegna's *Camera degli Sposi* frescoes (1465–74).

3 Piazza Broletto

Just north of the arcaded Piazza delle Erbe is this tiny square hemmed in by medieval buildings, including the 1227 *broletto* (town hall).

Duomo, Piazza Sordello

4 Piazza delle Erbe

Piazza delle Erbe *(below)* is a wonderfully jumbled, lively urban space, lined by arcades, filled with a food market each morning, and ringed by a fascinating assemblage of buildings.

5 Basilica di Sant'Andrea

Lodovico Gonzaga commissioned this basilica *(left)* in 1470 from Leon Battista Alberti, its façade a highly original take on Classicism. Mantegna is buried in the first chapel on the left.

6 Rotonda di San Lorenzo

This rotund church is a relic from an earlier age, built in 1082 and retaining scraps of medieval fresco in its otherwise pleasantly bare brick interior.

7 Teatro Scientifico Bibiena

This jewel-box of a late Baroque theatre is named after the architect who designed it, and was inaugurated in 1770 with a concert by Mozart, then a 13-year-old prodigy.

8 Palazzo d'Arco

This Neo-Classically remodelled *palazzo* from the Renaissance includes the 1520 Sala dello Zodiaco, frescoed with astrological signs, in an original 15th-century wing.

9 Casa del Mantegna

Mantua's most famous artist, Andrea Mantegna (1431–1506), custom-built this house-and-studio in 1465–74. It includes a circular courtyard *(left)* and a portrait of himself by his fellow-artist and friend Titian.

10 Palazzo Te

Giulio Romano's Mannerist masterpiece *(right)* is an ingenious interplay of spacious courts, sweeping building wings and discreet gardens. Built in 1525, it was frescoed largely by Romano.

Boat Tours

The Gonzagas widened the Mincio River, cupping their city within three defensive lakes. Lined by reeds, floating with white lotus, and now the protected homes of waterfowl and the highest concentration of fish in Italy, they're at their best in late May and June. You can take boat tours with Motonave Andes Negrini, Via San Giorgio 2 (0376-322-875) or Navi Andes (0376-324-506).

LV
BE
SI
DVS

Left **Pope Alexander III meets Barbarossa** Right **Benito Mussolini**

TOP 10 Moments in History

1 298–283 BC: Third Samnite War

The Po Valley and land to the north, once called Cisalpine Gaul, was a Celtic province that often found itself up against Rome. Its alliance with the Samnites failed, and Rome used the excuse to push its boundary north of the Po.

2 AD 313: Edict of Milan

During Rome's decline Milan became de facto capital of the Western Roman Empire. Constantine, holding court here in 313, made Christianity the official religion, setting a new course for European history.

3 572: Fall of Pavia to Lombards

In the 5th century barbarian tribes overran the disintegrating Roman Empire. Most came, sacked and left, but the Germanic Lombards took Pavia in 572 and settled in the Po Valley, expanding across the north. Eventually the Byzantines and Charlemagne trounced them, and the region dissolved into a network of city-states that lasted throughout the Middle Ages.

4 1176: Lombard League Defeats Barbarossa

When Swabian Emperor Frederick I (Barbarossa) levelled Milan and set up his own puppet mayors, the region's self-governing city-states banded together as the Lombard League and with papal support forced Barbarossa to return their autonomy.

5 1277: Ottone Visconti Defeats the Torriani

Archbishop Visconti overthrew the leading Torriani family in 1277. Under 160 years of Visconti rule, Milan extended its hegemony over much of the north.

6 1450: Francesco Sforza Comes to Power

The last Visconti died in 1447, leaving only an illegitimate daughter who couldn't inherit the title but was married to one Francesco Sforza. Milan's young Ambrosian Republic rashly hired Sforza to defend them from Venetian power-grabbers. Instead, he cut a deal with Venice, split up the territory and made himself duke.

Francesco Sforza comes to power in 1450

7 1499: The Sforza Cede Milan to France

Francesco's son Galeazzo Maria was murdered in 1476,

Previous pages **Leonardo's *Last Supper* (see pp8–9)**

after which power passed to Galeazzo's brother Lodovico, who was known as "Il Moro" ("The Moor") on account of his looks. Lodovico ushered the Renaissance into Milan, inviting the likes of Leonardo da Vinci to his court, but in 1499 ceded control to Louis XII. The city changed hands repeatedly until Austria seized power in 1706.

8 1848: Cinque Giornate Revolt

The 19th-century Risorgimento (unification movement) inspired the Milanese to rise up, on March 18, for five days, with their victory triggering the demise of Austrian rule. By 1859 King Vittorio Emanuele II controlled Lombardy: he sent General Garibaldi off to conquer the rest of the peninsula, forming a new kingdom – Italy.

9 1945: Mussolini Executed

Mussolini's fascist regime ended after his alliance with Hitler put Italy on the losing side of World War II. As the Allies drew closer Mussolini fled with his mistress. They were caught by partisans and shot on Lake Como, their bodies later strung up on Milan's Piazzale Loreto and stoned.

10 1990: Lombard League Wins Local Elections

Northern resentment of sharing wealth with the much poorer south found political expression in the Lombard League, a separatist party that came to prominence in 1990. Re-dubbed the Northern League, it espoused federalism and in 2001 gained power as part of the Forza Italia coalition (now known as Popolo della Libertà) led by media mogul and entrepreneur Silvio Berlusconi.

Top 10 Historical Figures

1 St Ambrose (334–97)
Milan's bishop put down the Arian heresy and helped establish Church autonomy.

2 St Augustine (354–430)
St Ambrose's star pupil – an African-born philosopher.

3 Theodolinda (500s)
Lombard queen who converted her populace to orthodox Christianity.

4 Gian Galeazzo Visconti (1378–1402)
This conqueror of vast territories was the first Milan ruler to gain the title of Duke.

5 Lodovico "Il Moro" Sforza (1452–1508)
"The Moor" ruled Milan's Renaissance court but ceded to France, later siding against the French and being exiled.

6 St Charles Borromeo (1538–84)
The crusading archbishop carried out Counter-Reformation ideals in the north.

7 Antonio Stradivari (1644–1737)
The greatest violin-maker who ever lived learned his craft in the city of Cremona.

8 Alessandro Volta (1745–1827)
This Como physicist invented the battery in 1800 and gave his name to the electrical unit.

9 Benito Mussolini (1883–1945)
Known as *Il Duce* (The Leader), Mussolini founded the Fascist Party in Milan in 1919, and ruled Italy from 1922 until 1943.

10 Silvio Berlusconi (b. 1936)
The founder of the Forza Italia party survived bribery scandals to become Italy's longest-serving prime minister.

Left **La Scala poster** Centre **Designer shopping** Right **Panini snacks at the bar**

Top 10 Lombard Experiences

Detail of the Duomo's rooftop

1 Exploring the Roof of Milan's Duomo

You can wander freely about the forest of Gothic carving adorning the rooftop of Milan's cathedral. Duck under the buttresses, skirt along the eaves and clamber onto the peaked roof of the nave to drink in a panorama across the city *(see pp10–11)*.

2 A Milanese Shopping Spree

Milan is a world capital of high fashion, home to dozens of the top designer names *(see pp58–9)* in its Quadrilatero d'Oro, or "Golden Rectangle" of streets *(see p57)*. Add in designer household objects, silk from Como, fine wines and foods, and Milan becomes a shopper's paradise.

3 Snacking on a Café Crawl

Between about 6pm and 9pm, many Milanese bars and cafés have Happy Hour when a cocktail costs between €7 and €15 and includes a substantial buffet spread with several courses (meat, fish or pasta). You can easily make a decent early dinner out of it.

4 An Evening on the Navigli

Milan's southern district of canals and warehouses has been converted to a lively evening area of restaurants, pizzerias, bars, pubs and funky shops *(see p94)*.

Cruise boat, Lake Como

Milan's Navigli district

5 A Night at the Opera

Italy's premier opera house, La Scala, has now emerged from extensive restoration, and you can again enjoy one of the world's best companies in a truly wondrous 18th-century setting *(see p74)*.

6 A Violin Concert in Cremona

In the city where Amati honed his craft and passed his skills to Stradivari, they take their fiddling seriously. Virtuosos from around the globe come to numerous festivals, concert seasons and trade fairs just for the chance to bow a few sonatas on the city's vast collection of original Strads *(see also p127)*.

Windsurfing on Lake Garda

7 A Cruise on Lake Como

The loveliest of the Italian lakes *(see pp106–113)* is best enjoyed from the waters. From this vantage point, devoid of traffic jams, you can see the glorious gardens and gracious villas lining its banks (from the road, all you may see is a high wall).

8 Sports on Lake Garda

The northern end of Lake Garda is buffeted by strong winds blowing down from the Sarca Valley in the north in the morning (the *sover*) and south up the lake in the afternoon (the *ora*). Together, they make for some of the best windsurfing and sailing conditions on any lake in Western Europe, and all summer long watersports fans flock from far and wide to Riva and its neighbour Torbole to thrash the waves *(see also p120)*.

9 Hill-Walking near the Lakes

Local tourist offices can often supply maps of mountain trails ranging from 15 minutes to two hours or more. Pick a point of interest as a goal: a ruined castle (Arco on Garda, Varenna on Como), medieval church (Madonna del Sasso above Locarno on Maggiore, San Pietro above Civate on Como), surging mountain stream (Fiumelatte by Lake Como's Varenna, Cascata del Varone above Riva del Garda), or prehistoric rock carvings *(below)*.

10 Seeking out the Region's Rock Carvings

The prehistoric Camuni tribes etched many rock faces in the pre-Alpine valleys of eastern Lombardy with curious figurative images and symbols. The oldest date back 11,000 years, while the most recent are medieval. Most carvings are in the Val Calmonica *(see p47)*. However, if you're on Lake Garda, detour at Torri del Benaco to the hillside hamlet of Crer, where a trail leads to some nice carvings.

Left **Casa degli Omenoni** Centre **Ca' Granda** Right **Entrance to the Galleria Vittorio Emanuele II**

TOP 10 Notable Milanese Buildings

1 Triennale (Palazzo dell'Arte)
On the outskirts of Parco Sempione, the Triennale houses Italy's first Design Museum, regular design and architecture exhibitions and an excellent decorative arts bookshop. The DesignCafé is worth a visit *(see p90)*.

Torre Velasca

2 Palazzo della Ragione
The arcade that takes up the ground level of this Lombard Romanesque palace, built in 1228–33 (the top floor dates from 1771), once hosted the city's main market. The relief on the façade depicts the 13th-century mayor Oldrado da Tresseno on horseback. Inside, the Salone dei Giudici has its original frescoes *(see p73)*.

3 Torre Velasca
When Nathan Rogers, Lodovico Belgioioso and Enrico Peressutti constructed this brick-red, 106-m (348-ft) tower block in 1956–8, they showcased their post-war engineering talents by extending the top nine floors beyond the lower ones on struts, much like an oversized medieval tower. Unfortunately, the maintenance costs have proved to be horrendous *(see p76)*.

4 Ca' Granda
In 1456 Francesco Sforza instituted one of his greatest public works, a massive hospital with separate wings for women and men, each based around four courtyards. The vast central Cortile Maggiore was added in the 17th century, along with the Annunciazione church with its Guercino altarpiece. The Neo-Classical men's wing was eventually completed in 1804; but the entire hospital moved elsewhere in 1939, to be replaced by the University of Milan in 1958 *(see p76)*.

5 Galleria Vittorio Emanuele II
High-class Italian elegance came to terms with the Industrial Age in such marvels of engineering as this four-storey shopping arcade roofed with a steel-and-glass canopy. It was built in

Galleria Vittorio Emanuele II

Palazzo is the Italian word for palace

1864–8 by Giuseppe Mengoni, who fell to his death from its scaffolding just days before the King arrived to open the galleria and lend it his name *(see p74)*.

6 Palazzo Marino

Milan's *comune* (city hall) has two distinct façades: a 1553 Mannerist one on Piazza S Fedele, and an 1886–92 Neo-Classical one facing La Scala theatre. The former was built by Galeazzo Alessi (who also designed the lovely main courtyard) in 1558; the latter dates to 1860 *(see p76)*.

7 Casa degli Omenoni

Renaissance sculptor Leone Leoni, whose works grace Milan's Duomo and Madrid's El Escorial, built this *palazzo* in 1565, lining the lower level of the façade with eight giant telamones – columns in the form of a male figure *(see p76)*.

8 Villa Necchi Campiglio

This perfectly preserved and restored 1930s villa has technology revolutionary for its time, including a heated pool and an internal phone system, testimony to the elegant Milanese inter-war lifestyle. It houses two important art collections: one of early 20th-century works; the other of 18th-century decorative arts *(see p88)*.

9 Pirelli Tower

Milan once had a rule about structures rising no higher than the golden Madonnina atop the Duomo *(see p11)*. The 127.1-m (417-ft) Pirelli Tower – designed in 1955–60 by a team headed by Gio Ponti and including Pier Luigi Nervi – broke that tradition, but placed a replica of the Madonnina on its own roof so she would still have the highest vantage point in Milan. It now houses Lombardy's regional government and in 2002 survived being struck by a small plane *(see p88)*.

Stazione Centrale

10 Stazione Centrale

Milan's massive railway station is often considered a remarkable example of Fascist-era architecture, though its design (of 1912) pre-dates this period and owes more to the Liberty style. Finally completed in 1931, the station is caked in gleaming white Aurisina stone and decorated with reliefs, statues and murals too often overlooked. *Piazza Duca D'Aosta*

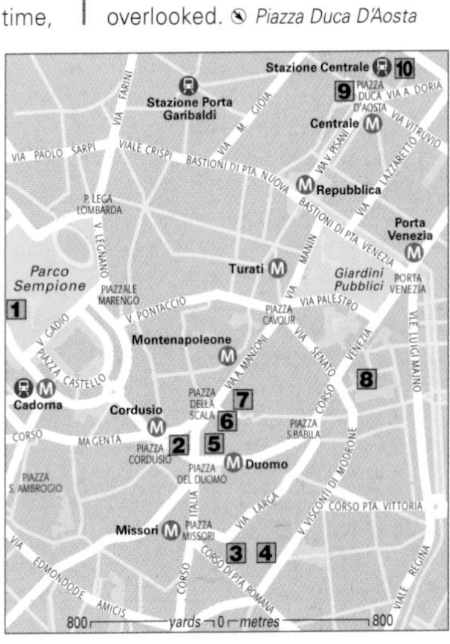

Left **Baptistry, Bergamo** Centre **Sant'Eustorgio, Milan** Right **Certosa di Pavia**

Top 10 Churches

1 Duomo, Milan

Milan's cathedral is the third-largest church in the world and a testament to Milanese persistence. Despite construction that lasted more than 400 years (1386–1813), it managed to remain uncompromisingly faithful to the original Gothic design, a beautiful structure of stone turrets, statues and flying buttresses *(see pp10–11)*.

Duomo, Milan

2 Sant'Ambrogio, Milan

St Ambrose himself, Milan's 4th-century bishop, inaugurated this church, which was overhauled in the 11th and 12th centuries. Highlights include a quiet entry atrium, Dark-Age mosaics glittering in the apse, and medieval features *(see pp20–21)*.

3 San Lorenzo Maggiore, Milan

Dating from the 4th century, this church is still pretty much Roman in its rotund design, although it was rebuilt several times in the Middle Ages. Inside the church are some of the oldest and best-preserved examples of post-Roman art in Northern Italy: 1,600-year-old Paleochristian mosaics *(see also p93)*.

4 Santa Maria delle Grazie, Milan

Each year, hundreds of thousands of people visit Leonardo da Vinci's *Last Supper* fresco in the adjacent refectory *(see pp8–9)*, but only a few bother with the lovely church itself. Make the effort, though, if you can: its architecture shows the stylistic changeover, from austere Gothic to Classical Renaissance, that marked the end of the 15th century. The art here is among Milan's best in sculpture, fresco and the rare *sgraffito* (etched designs) restored in the tribune *(see also p85)*.

Sant'Ambrogio, Milan

5 Santa Maria presso San Satiro, Milan

Though the main entrance is on Via Torino, walk around and up Via Speronari to see an 11th-century bell tower and the pretty exterior of a tiny Renaissance chapel. Turn right again on Via Falcone for the Renaissance-meets-Baroque rear façade finished in 1871. Here a secondary entrance is usually open, so you can nip inside to admire the 15th-century decorations *(see also p73)*.

6 Sant'Eustorgio, Milan

Ignore the insipid 19th-century façade, for the church behind it is ancient, founded in the 4th century. Beyond the main church and behind the altar is the cappella Portinari. It was designed locally, but so superbly did it embody early Renaissance Florentine ideals that it was for a long time attributed to Brunelleschi or Michelozzo. The chapel's masterpieces are the 1486 frescoes by Vicenzo Foppa *(see also p94)*.

7 Certosa di Pavia

Gian Galeazzo Visconti commissioned the construction of this vast, gorgeous Charterhouse in 1396 as a lavishly decorated home for a group of Carthusian monks, but more importantly to ensure his ruling clan would have a family burial chapel of grand proportions and extravagant artistic merit *(see p24–5)*.

Sant'Andrea, Mantova

8 Cappella Colleoni, Bergamo

Bartolomeo Colleoni was a *condottiere*, a redoubtable mercenary general who, as a reward for his services, received Bergamo as his own fiefdom. Never one for understatement, Colleoni demolished a church sacristy to make his own tomb, hiring the sculptor Giovanni Antonio Amadeo to decorate it with a complex allegory of Biblical and Classical reliefs plus a horse-mounted effigy of himself for the sepulchre inside *(see also p26)*.

Duomo, Como

9 Duomo, Como

Como's statue-studded cathedral is devoted to local patron and protector Sant'Abbondio, whose life is depicted in the giant gilt altarpiece of 1509–14. Other Renaissance tapestries and paintings – including one by Leonardo's protégé Bernardino Luini – grace the interior *(see also p107)*.

10 Basilica di Sant'Andrea, Mantova

Built to house a vial of Christ's blood, this basilica was created by some of Italy's finest architectural talents. Leon Battista Alberti, the great Renaissance theorist, designed it in 1470, Giulio Romano, a founder of Mannerism, enlarged it in 1530, and Baroque master Filippo Juvarra added the dome in 1732. Frescoes cover the barrel-vaulted interior *(see also p29)*.

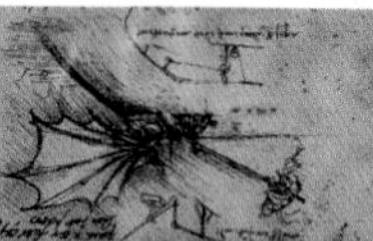

Left **Pinacoteca di Brera** Centre **Castello Sforzesco** Right **Museo Nazionale della Scienza**

Top 10 Museums

1 Pinacoteca di Brera, Milan

Lombardy's most important painting gallery, displaying works by Mantegna, Giovanni Bellini, Piero della Francesca, Caravaggio, Tintoretto, Veronese, Coreggio, Lotto, Carpaccio, Tiepolo, El Greco and Rembrandt *(see pp12–15)*.

2 Pinacoteca Ambrosiana, Milan

This formidable mix of Old Masters was started by Cardinal Federico Borromeo as an adjunct to the Ambrosiana Library. Famously, the library is home to the *Codex Atlantico*, which contains the lion's share of Leonardo's drawings and sketches – photocopied pages from it are displayed in the Pinacoteca. Elsewhere, you'll find paintings by Botticelli, Titian and Caravaggio, as well as Raphael's giant preparatory sketch for the *School of Athens* *(see pp18–19)*.

3 Castello Sforzesco, Milan

There's a bit of everything here: paintings by the likes of Bellini and Mantegna, a cycle of 16th-century tapestries, archaeological collections and, its greatest piece, Michelangelo's unfinished *Rondanini Pietà* *(see pp16–17)*. Entrance to the castle is free, but there is an entry fee for the Musei Civici within.

4 Museo Poldi-Pezzoli, Milan

Poldi-Pezzoli's mansion is preserved as a monument to his collections, from Persian tapestries, ancient arms and armour to historic jewellery and, above all, art. In one room alone, there are paintings by Piero della Francesca, Giovanni Bellini, Mantegna and Botticelli *(see p74)*.

5 Museo Nazionale della Scienza e della Tecnologia – Leonardo da Vinci, Milan

Had Leonardo possessed more technological ambition, we might have had working versions of his helicopters, water screws, gatling guns, parachutes and siege engines over four centuries ago. As it is, we can make do with the (modern) wooden mock-ups on display at this science and technology museum, alongside instructive exhibits on physics and antique autos and aeroplanes *(see p93)*.

Pinacoteca Ambrosiana, Milan

6 Civico Museo Archeologico, Milan

Among the top pieces in this small archaeological collection, which traces Lombard and neighbouring civilizations from prehistory to the end of the Roman era,

Set design by Giacoma Balla, Museo Teatrale alla Scala, Milan

is the Trivulzio Cup. This precious 4th-century glass cup has a delicate glass netting hovering just above the chalice surface on thin stilts of glass, along with a raised inscription that reads "Drink to Enjoy Long Life" *(see p85).*

7 Museo Teatrale alla Scala, Milan

If it has to do with the opera in Milan, it's on display here. It's an eclectic collection, from costumes worn by Nureyev or Callas to historic musical instruments, and from Verdi's death mask (and some of his original scores) to Toscanini's batons *(see p88).*

8 Galleria d'Arte Moderna – Villa Belgiojoso Bonaparte, Milan

This fine collection of art, housed in the handsome Villa Belgiojoso Bonaparte *(see p86),* includes Neo-Classicism and Romanticism works from the beginning of the 20th century. Italian 20th-century works can be seen in the Museo del Novecento *(see p73).*

9 Galleria dell'Accademia Carrara, Bergamo

Count Giacomo Carrara, a collector and expert on literature and art, left his collection to Bergamo, on his death in 1796. Today the gallery houses over 1,800 paintings, including works by Botticelli, Mantegna, Bellini and Raffaello. There is also a significant collection of prints and sketches, sculpture and china. Above all, though, come to admire the emotion-filled Renaissance paintings of Lorenzo Lotto, a Venetian painter who settled in Bergamo in 1513 *(see pp26–7).*

10 Museo di Santa Giulia, Brescia

Though there are Romanesque carvings and detached frescoes galore in the cloisters, chapels and chambers of this medieval monastery, the real focus here is on Brescia's great era as a Roman colony, and the archaeological works on display are astoundingly beautiful and well preserved *(see also p126).*

Botticelli's *Pietà* (1495), Museo Poldi Pezzoli

Left **The town of Bellagio on Lake Como** Right **Sirmione**

TOP 10 Lakeside Attractions

1 Isole Borromee, Lake Maggiore

This trio of islets off Stresa – two clad in gardens and palaces, the third with a fishing village – rank among the top 10 sights in the whole region *see (pp22–3).*

Rocca di Anghera

2 Santa Caterina del Sasso, Lake Maggiore

The façade and interior of this church perched just above the water are covered with decaying frescoes dating from the hermitage's foundation in the 13th century to its suppression by the Austrians in the 19th; the Dominicans returned in 1986. Be warned: there are many steps down from the car park, and the ferries servicing the ancient dock are infrequent. Look out on the loggia for a winch assembly once used with a basket to raise the daily shopping – and the occasional frail monk – from the boat decks *(see also p99).*

Santa Caterina del Sasso

3 Rocca di Angera, Lake Maggiore

This 8th-century Lombard fortress dominates Angera's headland. Expanded in the late 13th century by the Visconti of Milan, it later became the seat of its own county, and in 1449 passed to the Borromeo clan. Today the glowering fortress preserves delicate medieval frescoes and a Doll Museum *(see also p99).*

4 Bellagio, Lake Como

Perhaps the loveliest town on any of the lakes has it all: a harbourside arcade of cafés, sumptuous gardens surrounding stately villas, steep medieval alleys, and hotels and shops in all price ranges. The Romanesque church of San Giacomo has a 12th-century pulpit with reliefs of the Evangelists *(see also pp108 & 110).*

5 Como's Duomo, Lake Como

The exterior of Como's cathedral, begun in the late 14th century, is a festival of statues and bas-reliefs. Inside are Renaissance altarpieces and tapestries *(see p107)*.

Quiet alley in Varenna

6 Villa Carlotta, Lake Como

Owing its beauty and fame to three owners, the villa itself was begun in 1643 for Giorgio Clerici. In 1801 it passed to lawyer Gian Battista Sommariva, and he filled it with Neo-Classical sculptures and Romantic paintings. The former include *Palamede* by Canova and *Cupid and Psyche* by his student Tadolini; the latter a famed *Last Kiss of Romeo and Juliet* by Francesco Hayez, master of stolen-kiss scenes. In 1847 it passed to the Prussian Princess Carlotta, who lent it her name while her husband, Prince Giorgio di Sassonia-Meiningen, furnished it in Empire style. He also created the magnificent botanical gardens *(see pp44 & 108)*.

7 Varenna, Lake Como

Varenna is less touristy than Bellagio and almost as rewarding. It has a waterfront promenade, two small churches with medieval frescoes on the main square, two villas-with-gardens to wander, and the half-ruined Castello di Vezio high above town. Just south of Varenna, and only from March until October, the Fiumelatte gushes from the cliff face down about 250 m (800 ft) into the lake, making it the shortest river in Italy *(see also pp108–9 & 110)*.

8 Il Vittoriale, Lake Garda

An over-the-top Art Nouveau overhaul of this villa owned by the flamboyant poet, adventurer and national hero Gabriele d'Annunzio was financed by none other than Mussolini himself – basically as a bribe to silence d'Annunzio's criticism of the fascist government *(see also pp45 & 118)*.

9 Sirmione, Lake Garda

Jutting into the lake from the southern shore is a skinny peninsula. At its tip sits the postcard-perfect town of Sirmione, guarded by a striking castle complete with moat and drawbridge. It's a popular resort, with plenty of hotels and shopping, but also some fine little churches and the ruins of a Roman villa at the promontory's very tip *(see pp117 & 120)*.

10 Giardino Botanico Hruska, Lake Garda

Arturo Hruska, Swiss dentist to Europe's royalty in the early and mid-20th century, laid out these sumptuous botanical gardens between 1940 and 1971 *(see pp45 & 118)*.

A steep lane in picturesque Bellagio

Left **Borromeo Palace** Centre **Gardens, Villa Carlotta** Right **Terrace, Villa Monastero**

TOP 10 Villas and Gardens

1 Borromeo Palace, Lake Maggiore

The Borromeo family's 1670 *palazzo* on the lushly landscaped Isola Bella is an incomparable glimpse into the lifestyle of the wealthiest of Lombard families *(see p22)*.

2 Villa Taranto, Lake Maggiore

The villa at Verbania *(see p100)*, built in 1875 by Scotsman Neil MacEacharn, is closed to the public, but you can wander the landscaped gardens filled with exotic plants. Rare species include the world's largest water lily at 2 m (6 ft) across and the towering Metasequoia, which was believed extinct for 200 million years until found in China in 1941.

Via Vittorio Veneto, Pallanza, Verbania • Map A2 • 0323-556-667 • www.villataranto.it • 8:30am–6:30pm daily; last entry 5:30pm • Closed Nov–end Mar • Adm

3 Villa Carlotta, Lake Como

Lake Como is famous for its extravagant villas, but while some gardens are open, few of the buildings themselves can be visited. At Villa Carlotta, however,

Borromeo Palace and Lake Maggiore

Fountain, Villa Taranto

you can visit both the late Baroque villa filled with Neo-Classical statues and Romantic paintings, and the extensive, lush gardens *(see pp43 & 108)*.

4 Villa Serbelloni, Lake Como

The villa's private gardens cover the entire tip of the Bellagio promontory. The tours stick mainly to the paths, overlooking Italianate, English-style and Mediterranean sections. Stendhal described the vista from the top as "sublime and enchanting" – indeed, it's the only spot from which you can see down all three arms of Lake Como simultaneously *(see p108)*.

5 Villa Melzi, Lake Como

Francesco Melzi, the Vice-President of Napoleon's Cisalpine Republic, had this Neo-Classical villa built on Bellagio's southern edge. The villa is off-limits, but you can wander the gardens to the water's edge, visit a small museum (Etruscan, Egyptian and Roman artifacts) and see a mock Moorish temple that inspired a pair of Liszt piano concertos, written during the composer's stay here *(see p108)*.

6 Villa Monastero, Lake Como

Entrance, Villa Cipressi

The original structure was not really a monastery, but a Cistercian convent founded in 1208. It was disbanded by Charles Borromeo in the 16th century after he heard lascivious stories about its nuns. After centuries as a noble villa, it's now owned by a science research centre. You can visit a terrace of palms, cypresses, magnolias and roses, and a greenhouse of citrus trees *(see p108)*.

7 Villa Balbianello, Lake Como

Department store mogul and explorer Guido Monzino gave this 1784 villa and its gorgeous gardens to FAI (the Italian National Trust) in 1988. A museum inside chronicles his adventures from Mount Everest to the North Pole. The property topped the famous Como sights list after appearing in *Star Wars: Episode II* and *Casino Royale (see pp51 & 107)*.

8 Villa Cipressi, Lake Como

Fancy spending the night at one of Lake Como's gorgeous villas? The Cipressi is now a hotel, and guests can wander its cypress-shaded gardens, blooming with wisteria, for free *(see pp109 & 113)*.

9 Il Vittoriale, Lake Garda

This kitschy Art Nouveau villa was created by poet and adventurer Gabriele d'Annunzio, a flamboyant man who once flew a biplane over Vienna in 1918 to prove an invasion was possible, and in 1919 used private troops to take over a border town ceded to Yugoslavia, earning himself acclaim as a national hero and the enmity of those in power. The villa represents his life, loves and philosophy, which are cheerfully explained by guides. The famous plane is preserved in an outbuilding *(see p118)*.

10 Giardino Botanico Hruska, Lake Garda

Swiss dentist and naturalist Arturo Hruska may have had only a single hectare of lake property, but over 30 years he managed to turn it into a microcosm of Dolomite and Alpine flora. Since 1989, Austrian multimedia artist André Heller has kept it open it to the public *(see p118)*.

Villa Balbianello

Left **Pavia** Right **Vigevano**

TOP 10 Small Towns and Villages

1 Sabbioneta

An entire town planned between 1556 and 1591 to Renaissance ideals, Sabbioneta is the legacy of Vespasiano Gonzaga Borromeo, who, bereft of heirs, put his energies into a complex of palaces and a theatre *(see p127)*.

Crema

2 Crema

Though originally a fiercely loyal satellite of Milan, Crema's formative period was under the Venetians (1454–1797). It's a tidy town of white and pink marble façades, a delightful Duomo and a civic museum that includes scores by composer Francesco Cavalli.
Map E5 • Tourist info: Via Racchetti 8 • 0373-81-020 • www.prolococrema.it

3 Lodi

Built in 1158 after Barbarossa *(see p32)* razed the original town 5 km (3 miles) to the west, Lodi is celebrated for its Duomo and octagonal church of the Incoronata. The latter is slathered with frescoes, gilded stuccoes and fine paintings by Il Bergognone.
Map D5 • Tourist info: Piazza Broletto 4 • 0371-409-238 • www.turismo.provincia.lodi.it

4 Pavia

The capital of northern Italy in the Dark Ages is now lost in Milan's suburban sprawl but retains its historic centre. In addition to the glorious Certosa *(see pp24–5)*, other important churches include San Pietro in Ciel d'Oro and San Michele, both full of Romanesque carvings, and the Duomo, whose architects included Bramante and Leonardo. Pavia also boasts a Renaissance bridge and 14th-century castle with paintings by Antonella da Messina, Bellini, Correggio, Luini and Tiepolo.
Map C6 • Tourist info: Piazza della Vittoria • 0382-59-7001

Renaissance bridge, Pavia

Bormio

5 Vigevano

Lodovico "Il Moro" Sforza *(see p33)* was born in the castle that dominates this town of silk and shoe factories. The arcaded Piazza Ducale was designed by Bramante; the Baroque Duomo was built in 1680. ✆ *Map B5 • Tourist info: Via Merula 40 • 0381-690-269*

6 Castiglione Olona

In the 14th century Cardinal Branda Castiglione fell in love with the new Gothic painting style he saw in Florence and was determined to import it to his hometown. The ageing painter Masolino did some of his best works in the cardinal's palace and the Chiesa Collegiata. The Chiesa di Villa nearby is a Brunelleschian church with colossal saints flanking the entrance. ✆ *Map B3 • Tourist info: Piazza Garibaldi 1 • 0331-858-301*

7 Civate

The main town on little Lake Annone was a medieval stop for pilgrims visiting its 8th-century abbey, which was said to house a set of Saint Peter's Keys to Heaven (long-vanished). In the hills above town is the stunning Romanesque retreat of San Pietro al Monte *(see p110)*.

8 Chiavenna

This town in the Alpine valley is littered with *crotti* – caverns used to cure meats and cheeses – some of which have been converted into *osterie*. An old stone quarry above town is home to a botanical park; and the Parco Marmitte dei Giganti contains prehistoric carvings. ✆ *Tourist info: Piazza Caduti della Liberta • 0343-334-42 • www.valchiavenna.com*

9 Val Calmonica Villages

The villages of Capo di Ponte and Nadro di Ceto are the best access points for the prehistoric rock carvings found in the valley north of Lake Iseo. The images are at least 3,000 years old and include hunting scenes. ✆ *Tourist info: Via S Briscioli 42, Capo di Ponte • 0364-42-080 • www.invallecamonica.it*

10 Bormio

This year-round skiing village high in the Valtellina is equal parts high-class resort and medieval village. It's also a gateway to a park of glaciers, peaks, trails and gorgeous Alpine vistas. ✆ *Tourist info: Via Roma 131b • 0342-903-300 • www.valtellina.it*

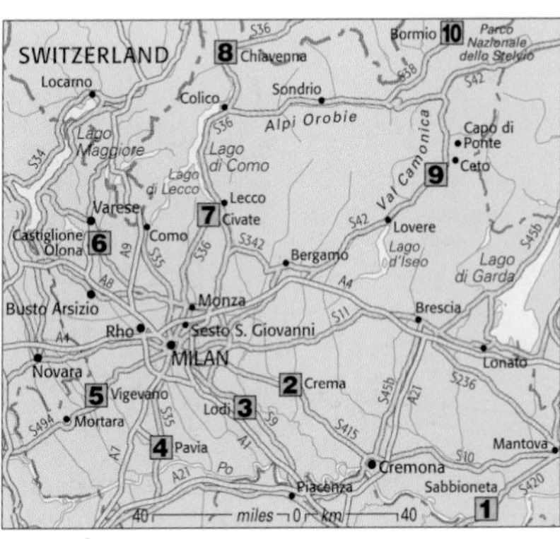

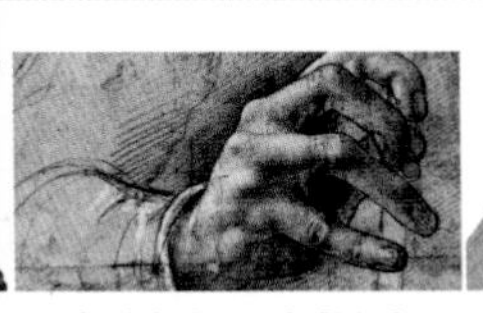

Left ***St Luke Polyptych* by Mantegna** Centre ***Study* by Leonardo** Right **A portrait of Caravaggio**

TOP 10 Artists Working in Lombardy

1 Andrea Mantegna (1431–1506)

Mantegna's classical mode of High Renaissance painting differed from but was as ethereally beautiful as that of his brother-in-law Giovanni Bellini. In 1460 he became court painter to the Gonzagas of Mantova, where he left masterful frescoes on the walls of the Palazzo Ducale *(see p28)*. Milan's Pinacoteca di Brera houses his remarkably foreshortened *Dead Christ (see p12)*.

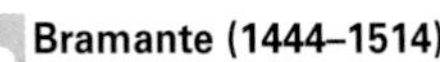

2 Bramante (1444–1514)

The great architect of the High Renaissance travelled from Urbino to Florence, then Milan and Rome, leaving churches in his wake (and doing a stint as chief architect of St Peter's in Rome). He favoured geometric designs and smooth walls, with architectural lines picked out in dark stone.

3 Leonardo da Vinci (1452–1519)

The ultimate Renaissance Man was a genius painter, inventor and scientist. His *sfumato* technique of blurring outlines and progressively hazing distances lent his works tremendous illusory depth. His inventions – including helicopters, machine guns and water systems – were centuries ahead of their time but mostly confined to sketches, though working models have now been built at Milan's technical museum. *(See pp8–9, 40 & 93.)*

***Self-portrait* by Leonardo da Vinci**

4 Bernardino Luini (1475–1532)

This apprentice of Leonardo was so taken with his master's talents that he spent his life churning out paintings in the Leonardo style without ever really developing one of his own.

5 Il Bergognone (1480–1523)

With the Renaissance raging all around him, Il Bergognone remained firmly a late Gothic painter, cranking out lovely but staid devotional paintings rooted in the style of his Milanese predecessor Vincenzo Foppa.

***Self-portrait* by Futurist Umberto Boccioni**

6 **Giulio Romano (1499–1546)**
Raphael's protégé helped finish his master's commissions after his death, but his fame as a frescoist was soon eclipsed by his architectural technique. Both came to the attention of the Gonzagas in Mantova, who commissioned from him the Palazzo Te *(see p29)* and other buildings. Only failing health kept him from returning to Rome to become chief architect of St Peter's.

7 **Giuseppe Arcimboldo (1527–93)**
This Milanese Mannerist was a gimmick artist, but very good at it. He churned out allegorical "portraits" that are actually collages: of flowers, fruit, fish, weapons, animals or even flames.

8 **Caravaggio (1571–1609/10)**
The Baroque master, who influenced an entire generation, used peasant models and a technique of heavy chiaroscuro, playing harsh light off deep black shadows to create dramatic scenes with brilliant realism.

9 **Francesco Hayez (1707–76)**
Born in Venice, Hayez moved to Rome – where he mixed with Ingres and Canova – then Milan, balancing his painting between the Romantic and Neo-Classical ideals of the age. He became director of the Pinacoteca di Brera.

10 **Umberto Boccioni (1882–1916)**
This leading Futurist was born in the south but soon moved to Milan. His failed journalism career served him in writing treatises on Futurism, while his paintings and sculptures were among the most admired of his era.

Top 10 Artistic Eras in Lombardy

1 **Ancient**
From prehistoric rock etchings dating back to the 12th century BC to sophisticated Roman villas of the 5th century AD.

2 **Lombard**
Lombard buildings from the 5th to 10th centuries feature triangular façades, blind arcades and ribbed vaulting.

3 **Romanesque**
A simple style of architecture in the 11th and 12th centuries defined by rounded arches and crude, expressive carvings.

4 **Gothic**
Pointed arches and flying buttresses allowed ceilings to soar in the 13th and 14th centuries. Painting became more expressive and realistic.

5 **Renaissance**
Classical architecture and elegant painting, with delicate colours and new techniques such as perspective (15th–16th centuries).

6 **Baroque**
The Renaissance but with profuse décor; big in the 17th century, then spiralled into overwrought Rococo in the 18th.

7 **Neo-Classical**
Late 18th to early 19th-century quest for the soul of the ancients; austere in style.

8 **Romantic**
A 19th-century return to the Gothic age and overwrought décor.

9 **Liberty**
The Italian Art Nouveau of the early 20th century delighted in asymmetrical organic curves.

10 **Futurist**
Italy's Cubism was obsessed with the modern world of the early 20th century.

Left **Film version of *I Promessi Sposi*** Right **Antonioni's *La Notte***

TOP 10 Books and Films Set in Lombardy

1 I Promessi Sposi (The Betrothed)
Written in the 1800s, Alessandro Manzoni's novel is a window into Lombard life in the 1600s, set in Milan and Manzoni's Lake Como hometown of Lecco during Spanish rule. It is required reading for all Italian schoolchildren and has been translated into many languages.

Rock Hudson and Jennifer Jones in the 1957 film of *A Farewell to Arms*

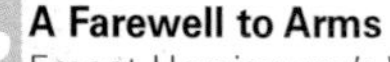

2 A Farewell to Arms
Ernest Hemingway's World War I novel (written in 1929) tells the story of an American soldier wounded while fighting for the Italian army. He convalesces in a Milan hospital, and, after inadvertently deserting while escaping the Germans, reunites with his love in Stresa on Lake Maggiore. They stay at the Des Iles Borromées hotel (where Hemingway himself often stayed) *(see p103)*, then flee by boat across to Swiss Locarno.

3 Twilight in Italy
The first place D H Lawrence and his lover Frieda settled during their European peregrinations was the shores of Lake Garda, during the winter of 1912–13. In 1916 he compiled his notes on those happy first months spent in Italy and wrote this travelogue.

4 A Month by the Lake
It's 1937, and a group of stodgy society Brits and bored Yanks loosen their mores and inhibitions on the shores of Lake Como. Vanessa Redgrave and Uma Thurman head up the cast of this 1995 film by John Irvin. You can visit its setting, the Villa Balbianello *(see p45)*.

5 Miracle in Milan
Vittorio de Sica's 1951 fable of a magical dove that grants wishes to the inhabitants of a Milan slum uses an early version of "special effects", bridging the popular Neo-Realistic style of Italy's post-war cinema with the era of magical realism in film-making that Fellini would make famous.

Vittorio de Sica's *Miracle in Milan*

6 **A Traveller in Italy**
H V Morton, who in his youth gained fame scooping the story of Tutankhamun's tomb discovery in the 1920s, became one of the 20th-century's best, if little-known, travel writers. His 1950s journey through Italy is an erudite combination of travelogue, history and wonderful prose, much of it surprisingly undated.

7 **La Notte**
Film director Michelangelo Antonioni takes the slow death of affection between a couple, masterfully played by Marcello Mastroianni and Jeanne Moreau, and sets it against a backdrop of rapidly industralizing Milan in 1960.

8 **Theorem**
Pier Paolo Pasolini's usual mix of sex, homosexuality and a communist critique on the emptiness of bourgeois life defines this 1968 film. Handsome stranger Terrence Stamp raises the libidos of a middle-class Milanese family, then further stirs up their lives by disappearing.

9 **The Spider's Strategem**
Before gaining international fame, Bernardo Bertolucci made this 1969 story of a dysfunctional family haunted by the fascist past. He set this psychological drama in the quirky town of Sabbioneta.

10 **Casino Royale**
The beautiful grounds of Villa Balbianello on Lake Como *(see pp45 & 107)* featured in this James Bond film in 2006. Fans can also check out the famous Villa Gaeta, the location for the last scene in the movie. This private house in Art Nouveau style lies between Menaggio and Dongo, and is best seen from the ferry boat.

Top 10 La Scala Premieres

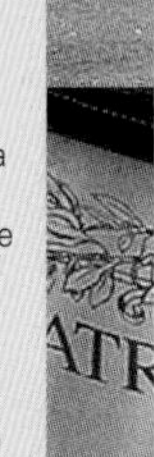

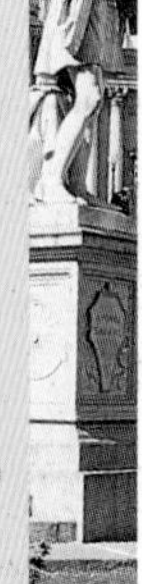

1 **L'Europa Riconosciuta (1778)**
Salieri's bellicose but light-hearted opera opened La Scala on 3 August 1778.

2 **La Pietra del Paragone (1812)**
Rossini's work signalled La Scala's shift from comic opera and Neo-Classical works to Romantic melodrama.

3 **Chiara e Serafina (1822)**
The first of many fun-loving Donizetti premieres.

4 **Norma (1831)**
Of Bellini's three La Scala premieres, the most famous is *Norma*, a Druid-Roman love triangle that ends badly.

5 **Nabucco (1842)**
Verdi would become La Scala's greatest home-grown composer, but he suffered two flops before this hit.

6 **Mefistofele (1868)**
Boito's first great success led to a collaboration with Verdi that produced *Otello* in 1887 and *Falstaff* in 1893.

7 **Aïda (1872)**
After a long absence from La Scala, Verdi offered this Egyptian melodrama.

8 **Madame Butterfly (1904)**
Puccini's tale of enduring love between a Japanese geisha and an American soldier.

9 **Turandot (1926)**
Puccini struck lucky again with exotic Asian fare – and, for once, a happy(ish) ending.

10 **The Rake's Progress (1951)**
Under Toscanini's direction, La Scala started opening up to foreign works, including this Stravinsky classic.

For more on La Scala – the world's greatest opera house – **see p74**

Left **Sagra del Carroccio** Right **Festa dei Navigli**

Top 10 Festivals and Events

1 Carnival

Carnevale in Milan is a combination of religious pomp, fancy-dress parade and Bacchanalian bash. Whereas carnivals elsewhere in the world – everywhere from Rio to Venice – end on Martedì Grasso ("Fat Tuesday"), Archbishop St Ambrose decreed that in Milan the party should go on until the following Saturday. No wonder they made him a saint. *Feb/Mar (ends the first Sat of Lent) • Info: 02-7740-4343*

2 Fashion Week

Milan is invaded by models, buyers, journalists and photographers four times a year. In mid-January and late June they come for menswear collections, while late February and late September are for womenswear. Taxis, hotel vacancies and restaurant tables get scarce, so visitors should plan ahead.

3 Palio di Legnano

Two years after the Lombard League trounced Barbarossa in 1176 *(see p32)*, the town of Legnano began celebrating the victory. Over 800 years later they're still at it, putting on a display of pageantry that ends with a horse race between the town's eight *contrade* (districts). *Last Sun in May • Info: Ufficio Palio del Comune • Piazza S Magno 9 • 0331-471-297*

Fashion Week

4 Festa dei Navigli

Milan's trendy Navigli canal district celebrates the start of summer on the first Sunday in June by bursting into a street fair with artisan stalls and live music. *First Sun in Jun*

5 Ferragosto

August 15, the Feast of the Assumption, is the day most Italians head to the beach or lakes for a two-week holiday, and life in the city comes to a halt. Mantua has a 15 August celebration of street artists, but Milan virtually shuts down. Only the restaurants and bars of the Navigli stay open. *15–31 Aug*

6 Stresa Festival, Stresa

Lake Maggiore's gateway to the Borromean Islands *(see p99)* hosts five musical weeks of concerts in venues throughout town and up and down the lake shores. *Late Aug–early Sep • Info: Via Carducci 38 • 0323-31-095 • www.stresafestival.eu*

7 Grand Prix, Monza

The biggest Formula One race of the year takes place in mid-September. At other times, you can still watch macho men driving cars at mind-boggling speeds from April through to October. *Grand Prix: 2nd weekend in Sep • Info: Via Vedano 5 • 039-24-821 • www.monzanet.it*

8 Stringed Instruments Festivals, Cremona

The home of Amati and Stradivarius celebrates luthiers and musicians in a series of festivals, concerts, exhibitions and international competitions *(see also pp35 & 127)*. ⊗ *Late Sep–early Oct • Info: Fondazione Antonio Stradivari, Piazza S Omobono 3 • 0372-801-801 • www.fondazionestradivari.it*

9 Milan Furniture Fair

Hotels are fully booked when the Salone Internazionale del Mobile, or Milan Furniture Fair, takes the stage in mid-April. Be sure to book early if you want to be present for the six days when the entire city comes alive with exhibitions and events related to the latest trends in furniture and interior design. ⊗ *Mid-April • Fieramilano Rho, Milan • 02-4997-1 • www.fieramilano.it*

10 Opera Season

La Scala *(see p74)* is the most important opera house in the world, and if you ever doubted opera was art, a night at its 18th-century home will help you transcend all doubt. The season opens on 7 December – the feast day of Milan's patron saint, Ambrose – and is a momentous occasion in the Milanese social calendar. ⊗ *Info: 02-7200-3744 • tickets: 02-860-775 • www.teatroallascala.org*

La Scala

Spectator Sports and Sporting Activities

1 Football (Soccer)

Lombardy boasts three Serie A teams, two of them in Milan *(see pp62–3)*. San Siro stadium is the main venue *(see p88)*.

2 Car Racing

The track at Monza, one of Europe's best, hosts the Italian Grand Prix in September (entry 7 opposite).

3 Horse Racing

Milan's Ippodromo *(see p88)* is the place to go for a flutter at the races.

4 Windsurfing

Stiff winds at the northern ends of the lakes make for some of the best lake windsurfing in Western Europe.

5 Cycling

Whether speeding down the Mincio Valley, mountain-biking, or ambling along the lakeside roads, Lombardy is great on two wheels.

6 Sailing

The same breezes that fuel windsurfers are enjoyed by sailors, especially on Lakes Garda, Como and Iseo.

7 Horse Riding

The hills and valleys around Lake Maggiore provide the best terrain for saddling up *(see also p111)*.

8 Hiking

Take a bracing trek into the hills above the lakes.

9 Golf

The luxury hotels of the lakes have all invested in designer golf courses *(see also pp111 & 121)*.

10 Skiing

In their northern reaches the lakes are bound by Italian pre-Alps that provide good skiing opportunities.

Following pages **Lake Maggiore's Isola Bella**

RISTORANTE MAGNO

Left **Versace shop front** Centre **Antiques, Via Montenapoleone** Right **Moschino, Via della Spiga**

TOP 10 Shopping Meccas in Milan

1 Via Manzoni

This broad boulevard became an epicentre of Milanese fashion when Giorgio Armani opened his gargantuan superstore here in 2000 *(see p77)*. On Manzoni there's everything from the Roman fashions of Davide Cenci (No. 7) to the check-me-out jewellery of Donatella Pellini (No. 20). *Map M2–3*

2 Galleria Vittorio Emanuele II

Milan's glorious 19th-century shopping mall *(see p74)*, though small, manages to host a little of everything. You'll find both the pinnacle of class (Prada) and the joys of mass-market culture (a Ricordi/Feltrinelli superstore of CDs and books). For a shopping break, visit the home-grown bastion of *la dolce vita* that is Zucca in Galleria *(see p80)*. *Map M3*

Prada, Via Montenapoleone

3 Corso Vittorio Emanuele II

This thoroughly modernized pedestrian street at the back of the Duomo is lined with arcades and some of the hippest shops in central Milan, including sophisticated brands like Furla (bags), Pollini (shoes) and Max Mara embodying international cutting-edge chic for young fashionistas. *Map M4–N3*

4 Via P Verri

Fashion-conscious men should head for Via P Verri, where they'll find a wonderful little boutique for the immaculately tailored Canali's suits at No.1, and Etro fragrances at the corner of Via Bigli. *Map M–N3*

5 Via Montenapoleone

Rodeo Drive, Fifth Avenue, rue du Faubourg-St-Honoré...

Galleria Vittorio Emanuele II

none can claim the hometown boutiques of Prada, Armani, Versace and more. Via Montenapoleone – "Montenapo" to its friends – is the main artery of Milan's Quadrilatero d'Oro, a "Golden Rectangle" of streets where the top international names in high fashion congregate alongside the best antiques and art dealers and a few classy cafés. *Map M2–N3*

Via della Spiga

6 Via Borgospesso

In the Quadrilatero d'Oro, this street has the highest concentration of art and antique shops, from lacquered 17th-century Venetian boxes at Silva (No. 12) to a bit of everything at Silbernagl *(see p79)*. *Map M–N2*

7 Via della Spiga

For sheer shopping volume and absolute delight, head to Via della Spiga, which has more worthy shops than any other street in all of Milan. Here's just a sample of the well-known names on offer here: Dolce e Gabbana (2, 26), Gherardini (8), Tiffany & Co. (19a), Krizia (23), Roberto Cavalli (42), Sermoneta Gloves (46) and Marni (50). *Map N2*

8 Corso Buenos Aires

This long road is where your average Milanese heads to shop, offering more than 350 shops in no particular order. You'll find everything from handmade men's dress shirts and Richard Ginori china to bootleg records. *Map P1*

9 Via San Gregorio

The grid of streets southeast of Milan's Stazione Centrale train station is Milan's best-kept shopping secret. Over 100 clothing warehouses and distributors pepper Via San Gregorio, Via Boscovich, Via C Tenca and others, offering cut-price goods.

10 Milan's Markets

The main market is Saturday's Fiera di Senigallia on Via Valenza, behind Porta Genova station. Milan's Sunday flea market surrounds the San Donato metro stop in the south. Local markets are on Via San Marco (Mon & Thu), Via Benedetto Marcello (northeast of the Giardini Pubblici) on Tuesdays, and Viale Papiniano in the Navigli (Tue & Sat). Markets tend to shut by 1pm, except on Sat. *Maps J6 (Via Valenza), M1 (Via San Marco), J5 (Papiniano)*

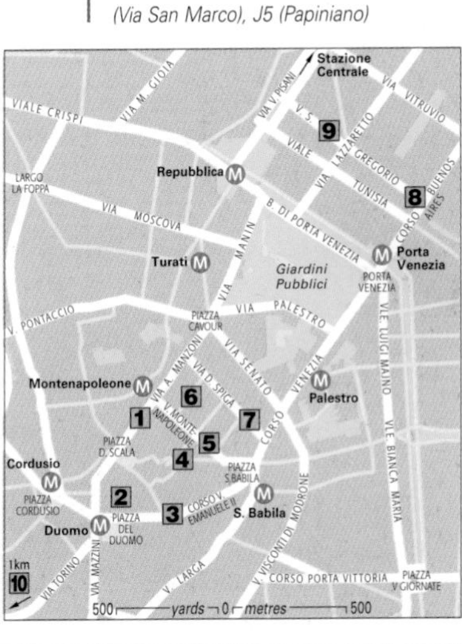

For the best individual shops in Milan, **see pp77–9, 89 & 96**

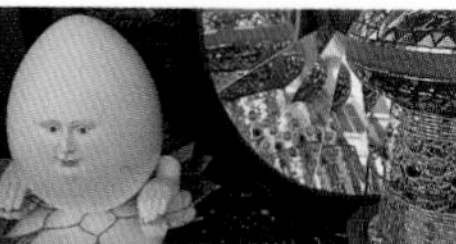

Left **English-language bookshop** Centre **Jewellery display, Via della Spiga** Right **Objets d'art**

Top 10 What to Buy

1 Designer Clothes

Milan, of course, is monumentally important to the world of fashion. Every important fashion label, whether local or based in Paris, New York or Florence, maintains a boutique in Milan. For those whose tastes outstrip their budgets, Milan is also home to some excellent stock shops and discount outlets.

Prada shoes and bags

2 Shoes

Italian shoes range from the practical to the gorgeous and outrageous. Some will last you a lifetime; some are just for very special occasions. All the famous labels offer lines of shoes, but you'd do best to seek out the specialists, whether it be a haute-couture work of art at Ferragamo *(see p78)*, a mass-produced Italian brand name or a designer bargain from Rufus *(see p89)*.

3 Handbags

Swoon over the designs from Prada and Bottega Veneta, or the slightly less pricey Coccinelle. Or, plump for one of the many well made, non-label leather bags, still in great Italian style.

4 Design Objects

Italian industrial designers are maestros at turning everyday objects such as kettles, lighting systems and juicers into works of art. The often whimsical, usually beautiful and always ergonomically sound results are on sale throughout Italy, or you can go right to the source on Lake Orta. Here, an artisan tradition gave rise in the late 19th century to firms such as Alessi, Bialetti and Lagostina.

5 Linens

Bassetti and Frette offer affordable, stylish linens. The haute couture of sheets and tablecloths is represented by Pratesi and, at the pinnacle, Jerusum, which provided the lace-edged linens for Italy's royal family in the 19th century.

6 Silk

Como has long been Italy's chief purveyor of finely spun silk fabrics. The Milanese maestros of haute couture come to Como to finger the fabrics that will soon be draped across a supermodel's shoulders. These same sought-after silks are available to the public in factory warehouses around Como and in shops across Lombardy.

7 Art and Antiques

Milan's art dealers offer a rich collection of lesser-known Byzantine and Baroque works and a plethora of 19th-century oils and other relatively affordable works of art. You'll find an

Italy's celebration of la dolce vita, *the art of living well, is nowhere more apparent than in its range of beautiful things to buy*

embarrassment of 18th-century Venetian chairs, country-style hardwood dressers and Empire-style clocks cluttering the *antichità* shops.

8 Wine
Lombard wines are generally excellent *(see p67)*. Furthermore, the lakes border both the Veneto – home to Valpolicella, Pinot Grigio and Soave – and Piemonte, where the mighty Barolo, Barbera and Barbaresco reds are crafted.

9 Books
A catalogue of Milanese galleries, a glossy tome of lake scenes or a translation of local literary classic *I Promessi Sposi (see p50)* might be a more treasured souvenir than a sheaf of postcards or trinkets.

10 Jewellery
Though it's not a top European capital of baubles and precious gems, Milan's jewellers hold their own. Seek out the bold creations of Donatella Pellini or the cutting-edge minimalism of Xenia. For something more classic, try Gobbi 1842 and especially Mario Buccellati, a firm that since 1919 has produced exquisite jewellery, elegant tableware and renowned silver *objets d'art*.

Antique glassware, Via Montenapoleone

Top 10 Fashion Houses and Gurus

1 Armani
Italy's top fashion guru is the master of smart clothes that, for a price tag with far too many zeroes, can help anyone look like a model.

2 Versace
Made "violently elegant" designs popular and costumed many La Scala productions in the 1980s.

3 Prada
The most chillingly expensive of Milan designers, Prada breathed new life into relaxed minimalism with the help of a small red stripe.

4 Mila Schön
A giant of fashion who pioneered the double-face fabric in the 1960s.

5 Krizia
Ever an eclectic designer, Mariuccia "Krizia" Mandelli has been flouting trends and winning awards since 1954.

6 Ermenegildo Zegna
Fourth-generation, environmentally-aware firm that uses the finest cashmere, merino and mohair in its fabrics.

7 Moschino
An *enfant terrible* of Milan's fashion scene since 1983.

8 Missoni
This husband-and-wife team has charmed the fashion world since 1953 with its multi-coloured, zigzag knitwear.

9 Trussardi
Founded by a Bergamasco glove-maker in 1910, Trussardi produces classic cuts and gorgeous leather accessories.

10 Ferré
The late Gianfranco Ferré was famous for "architectural" fashion, a look that lingers on in clothing and accessories.

For the top Milanese fashion boutiques in the city centre **see p77**

Left **Auditorium di Milano** Right **Alcatraz**

TOP 10 Entertainment Venues in Milan

1 La Scala
Housed in a glorious 18th-century theatre, this is Milan's – indeed, one of the world's – top opera companies, where Verdi was once house composer, Callas formerly graced the stage and costumes are designed by top fashion names. The season runs from December until May and tickets are scarce. It is advisable to book early *(see p74)*.

2 Scimmie
Part bar, part restaurant and part jazz club that doesn't limit itself to jazz. Since 1971, "Monkeys" has been shaking up the Navigli nightlife scene with live music daily until late in the night *(see p96)*.

3 Auditorium di Milano
Since 1999, and under the guidance of conductor Riccardo Chailly, the "Giuseppe Verdi" Symphony Orchestra of Milan has played in this re-invented 1930s' cinema, which stood derelict for decades after World War II. The orchestra boasts a repertoire ranging from Bach to 19th-century symphonic music and contemporary pieces. *Via S Gottardo 39 • www.laverdi.org*

4 Limelight
This is high-tech night-clubbing, with TV screens, Internet feeds, concerts broadcast live and a magnetic card that keeps track of your tab (you pay when you leave). The music ranges from modern pop and hip-hop to 1960s and 1970s revival – the owners are a group of Serie A footballers who are often seen here when not on the field *(see p96)*.

5 Magazzini Generali
Cavernous Magazzini Generali is a little bit of everything. It has a stage and auditorium that seats 1,000 for live acts, it can become a huge disco, it has a gallery for exhibitions, and it fits in live poetry readings and more besides. *Via Pietrasanta 14 • 02-5521-1313*

La Scala

6 Old Fashion Cafe
This veteran of the Milan nightlife scene remains popular, judging by the crowds hanging around outside waiting to get past the velvet rope. Situated in the

Magazzini Generali

Palazzo dell'Arte in Parco Sirmione, it has an elegant restaurant and a cosy lounge, both with dance floors. In summer the crowd spills out into the large garden. *Viale E. Alemagna 6 • 02-805-6231*

7 Black Hole

This huge nightclub, with three dance floors and stages for live acts, is open three nights a week. Wednesday is "Night Noir", an alternative night with live music and clubbing until dawn. On Fridays, DJ Max Martin spins a combination of 90s pop and house; Saturdays feature a popular 1980s revival night. *Viale Umbria 118 • 0349-466-9374 • www.blackholemilano.com*

8 Blue Note

The first European outpost of the famed New York jazz club serves up dinner and top-line performers Tuesday to Saturday and a jazz brunch on Sundays. The line-up is wide-ranging. Past performers have ranged from Bill Evans and Suzanne Vega to the London Community Gospel Choir. Booking is essential *(see p90)*.

9 Hollywood

This stalwart from the 1980s still offers you the best chance in all of Milan to spot a genuine international supermodel, making Corso Como one of the city's most fashionable streets. Though a perfectly standard discotheque from 1986, glitzy Hollywood continues to draw the most beautiful people in town, so dress to impress *(see p90)*.

10 Alcatraz

Located on a street that features a number of hip nightspots, Milan's biggest club is housed in a converted industrial space and hosts live music concerts, events and parties. The action begins around 11pm and goes on until about 3am. There is often live music during the week and dancing every Saturday and Sunday. The top bands visiting Milan play here *(see p90)*.

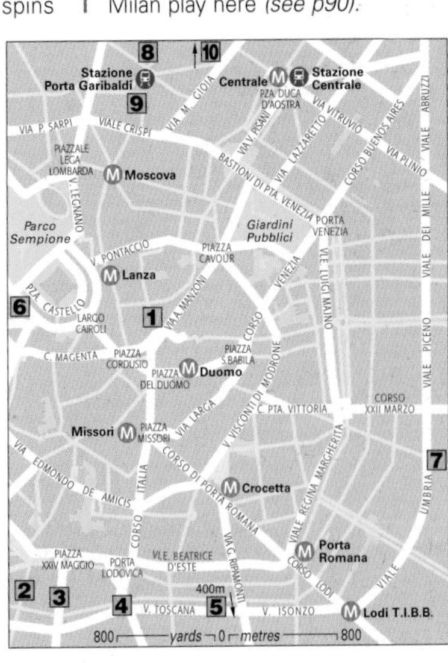

Left **Cycling in Mantua** Right **Gardaland theme park**

TOP 10 Attractions for Children

1 Exploring Milan's Duomo

Milan's cathedral is a Gothic wonderland of flying buttresses, soaring pinnacles, saintly statues, spiral staircases and hideous gargoyles – fun to explore for kids aged 5 to 95 *(see pp10–11)*.

2 The Best Science Museum in Italy

Milan's Museo Nazionale della Scienza e della Tecnologia has the usual impressive collection of a major science museum – historic cars, TV sets, steam engines, a planetarium and (in the Naval Museum upstairs) thousands of model ships – and Leonardo. The Renaissance genius "invented" (at least on paper) everything from helicopters to labour-saving mechanical devices. Full-scale models help bring his visions to life and may just help pique a youngster's interest in the Renaissance *(see pp40 & 93)*.

3 Puppet Shows

Italy's rich tradition of puppet shows, from Sicily's epic tales of Saracen warriors and Charlemagne's knights to Naples' slapstick Pulcinella (Punch and Judy) shows, has almost died out. Thankfully, here and there master puppeteers such as Cosetta and Gianni Colla at Milan's Teatro delle Marionette keep the tradition alive and update the stories to appeal to a modern audience.

Gelato **(ice cream)**

Teatro della Quattordicesima, Via Oglio 18, Milan • 02-552-113000 • www.teatrocolla.org • Oct–Apr

4 Acquario Civico

The Civic Aquarium's 36 huge tanks house around 100 species of fish, crustaceans, molluscs and echinoderms found in the Mediterranean and in Italian lakes and rivers. There are also many species of rare tropical fish, including piranahs, on view.

Via Gadio 2 • Map K2 • 02-8846-5750 • www.acquariocivicomilano.eu • 9am–1pm, 2–5:30pm Tue–Sun

5 Gelato Breaks

Italy's *gelato* puts all other ice creams in the world to shame. There are dozens of classic parlours around Milan, including Grom (Via Santo Margherita 4), Bastianello (Via Borgogna 5) and Grasso (Viale Doria 17). Look for the sign *"produzione propria"*, indicating that it's home-made. The true litmus test is to look for natural colours: you want banana that's naturally (if unappetizingly) grey, not bright yellow.

6 Football for Young Fans

An emotion-packed *calcio* (football) match at Milan's striking San Siro stadium *(see p88)* is fun for sports fans of all ages. And with two Serie A teams – FC Internationale (Inter) and AC Milan – the chances of catching a top-flight match during the season are excellent. Check out their websites for game schedules, or the Lega-Calcio website for information on Lombardy's other two Serie A squads, Como and Brescia. Alternatively, the Inter-Milan Museum (Gate 14, San Siro) comprises a visit to the stadium and the changing rooms. *www.inter.it • www.acmilan.com • www.lega-calcio.it*

7 Gardaland

Italy's top theme park, by Lake Garda, is a far cry from Disneyland, but it does have roller coasters, a jungle safari and a thrilling water park *(see p117)*. It's a place where older children can be dropped off for a day of fun while the parents drive off to explore those "boring villas and gardens" the kids are probably complaining about right now.

8 Windsurfing Lessons on Lake Garda

Garda is near perfect for all levels of surfers. There's enough wind to satisfy the experienced, but since the lake waters are relatively calm for most of the time, even novices can get out there and learn the techniques.

9 Lakeside Castles

You can relive the Middle Ages by exploring Lombardy's castles, scrambling up watch-towers and patrolling the ramparts like a soldier of old. The Castello Sforzesco in Milan *(see pp16–17)* is mostly a museum, though regular tours take you up onto the battlements. Those on the lakes can be more atmospheric, some with intriguing museums, others romantically half in ruins. The best fortresses are at Varenna *(see p110)*, and Arco, Malcésine and Sirmione *(see p117)* by Lake Garda.

Windsurfing on Lake Garda

10 Cycling in Mantua

The city of Mantua is flat, virtually surrounded by lakes and plains that stretch up and down the Mincio River, all of it begging to be explored on two wheels. It's a welcome break from all the churches and museums that can numb even an avid art fan, and a chance to delve into the more physical side of Italian culture.

Rocca Scagliera at Sirmione, by Lake Garda

Left **Cova, Milan** Centre **Caffè del Tasso, Bergamo** Right **I Portici del Comune, Cremona**

TOP 10 Cafés and Wine Bars

1 Zucca (Caffè Miani), Milan

Verdi and Toscanini would stop by after La Scala shows and King Umberto I declared that it served the best coffee in Milan. It even shows up in Boccioni's *Riot in the Galleria (see p12)*. This café opened inside the Galleria Vittorio Emanuele II *(see p56)* in 1868, though the Art Nouveau décor came a little later. Its prime location at the galleria entrance gives a great view of the Duomo façade *(see p80)*.

Caffè Zucca, Milan

2 Cova, Milan

The Faccioli family opened Cova near La Scala theatre in 1817 and, though it was later moved to Milan's prime shopping street, Via Montenapoleone, it has remained in the family – and continues to be café of choice for the city's elite. Its home-made pastries, chocolates and sandwiches are some of the most exquisite in town, and they brew up a mean cappuccino to boot. There's an elegant little tea room with refined service if all the window shopping has left you too tired to stand, but since this is still Italy, you're also welcome to just run in and toss back an espresso *(see p80)*.

3 Sant'Ambroeus, Milan

Looking every inch the 1936 café, from its wood-panelling to its pink stucco decorations, Sant'Ambroeus is counted among the great temples of chocolate in Italy. Their speciality is the *ambrogiotti*: an indulgence of dark chocolate wrapped around an egg cream *(see p80)*.

Cova, Milan

Pasticceria Marchesi, Milan

4 Il Marchesino alla Scala, Milan

The brainchild of chef Gualtiero Marchesi, credited for master-minding Italian creative cuisine, this bar-restaurant within La Scala opera house includes a sushi bar from where you can watch the action in the kitchen. *Piazza della Scala 2 • Map M3 • 02-7209-4338*

5 Bar Jamaica, Milan

This historic Milanese café in the Brera district has long been a haunt of artists, writers and intellectuals. It is also where Mussolini used to read (and correct) articles about himself in the daily newspaper, over a cappuccino. Bar Jamaica is busy at all hours, serving drinks from coffee to cocktails, as well as huge salads and hot and cold dishes. *Via Brera 32 • Map L2 • 02-876-723*

6 Bar Magenta, Milan

A lovely corner café that's a cross between an Irish pub and a Parisian Art Deco café, with a zinc bar, high ceilings, free newspapers and a decent list of dishes along with coffee, beer, cocktails and apéritifs *(see p90)*.

7 Pasticceria Marchesi, Milan

A wonderful old-fashioned café and pastry shop happily "discovered" by many a visitor trekking out to see the *Last Supper*. The decor hasn't changed since 1824, the coffee is quite good and the pastries are favoured by Giorgio Armani *(see p90)*.

8 Caffè Bolla, Como

Located just behind the Duomo, this long-established café is open all day serving freshly baked croissants for breakfast, pastries and ice cream. Considered the best in town for hazelnut, pistachio and chocolate flavours, Bolla has a faithful following, from both locals and visitors *(see p128)*.

9 Caffè del Tasso, Bergamo

For over 500 years, the Tasso has been Bergamo's meeting spot for everyone from princes to rebels. Garibaldi and his red shirts met here in revolutionary days; in fact, it was once such a hotbed of discontent that a decree (displayed on the wall) was made in 1845 prohibiting rebellious conversations here. *(see p128)*.

10 I Portici del Comune, Cremona

You just can't get a better seat in town than one at an outdoor table set under a lofty medieval arcade with the façade of Cremona's Duomo filling up your panorama. The coffee is good (not always a given), as are the *panini* and *gelato (see p128)*.

Il Marchesino alla Scala

Left **Place setting, Bellagio** Centre **Regional cheeses** Right **Fried slices of polenta**

TOP 10 Culinary Highlights of Lombardy

1 Cotoletta alla Milanese
For proof that the Lombards are Germanic at heart, look no further than Milan's archetypal dish, a breaded veal cutlet which is similar to *wienerschnitzel*.

2 Ossobuco
Succulent veal chops, cut across the shin bone, dredged in flour, lightly fried, then slow-cooked in wine and tomatoes with a bit of lemon-parsley-garlic *gremolata* tossed on top. Proper *ossobuco* is served on the bone (its very name means "bone-hole", though that sounds better in Italian): digging out the rich marrow is an integral part of enjoying the dish.

3 Polenta
Northern Italy's corn-meal side dish can be prepared in any form, from a creamy texture to a paste firm enough to slice and fry. It is often topped with mushrooms or some other delicacy.

4 Risotto alla Milanese
If you order risotto in Italy, you usually have to wait at least 20 minutes as the cook must constantly stir the rice until it reaches the perfect texture. It is time-consuming to make in small batches, so some restaurants will prepare it only for two or more people. In Milan, they often tinge their risotto bright yellow with saffron, and may throw in seasonal vegetables. In Mantua, they usually spice it up with sausage.

Cotoletta alla ilanese

5 Tortelli di Zucca
Mantua specializes in this slightly sweet first course, stuffing pockets of fresh pasta with a rich pumpkin paste. It's customarily topped with a simple butter and sage sauce.

6 Strangolapreti
They're called "priest-stranglers" because these little balls of ricotta and spinach are deemed so rich they'd choke a poor prelate's simple palate. Usually served with butter and grated parmesan, though sometimes with tomato sauce.

Risotto with fish

7 Cassoeûla
Somewhere between a soup, a stew and a main course, this mighty Milanese dish throws

Cassoeûla

sausage and chunks of pork into a thick cabbage soup, with polenta on the side. It'll stick to your ribs (and clog your arteries).

8 Lake Fish

Several fish favourites are plucked daily from Lombardy's lakes. The best include *persico* (perch), *lavarello* (a whitefish), *trota* (trout), *luccio* (pike), *coregone* (another whitefish) and *tinca* (tench).

9 Cheeses

Lombardy is the land of Italy's king of blue-veined cheeses, gorgonzola, and its lesser-known cousin taleggio (no mould, just strongly-odoured goodness). It is also home to Parmesan cheese: grana padano, parmigiano reggiano and grana lodigiano. On the milder end of the scale are the popular bel paese and the spreadable and creamy marscarpone.

10 Panettone

All across Italy at Christmas time people snap up boxes of this traditional Lombard cake, though locals enjoy it year-round. It is quite dry, and studded with fruit and candied peel.

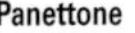
Panettone

Top 10 Wines

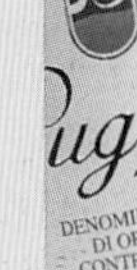

1 Bardolino

This wine is a light, balanced red from Lake Garda's Veneto shore.

2 Valtellina

This meaty red from the hills of Lake Como is powerful: one type is named "Inferno".

3 Franciacorta

South of Lake Iseo, Italy's only DOCG sparkling wine; try Saten. Also red (Cabernet-Merlot) and white (Chardonnay-Pinot) DOCs.

4 Lambrusco

Thick, dark, fizzy red from Mantua. Cheap but delicious; great with pizza.

5 Oltrepò Pavese

Also slightly fizzy, lighter and tangier than Lambrusco. The Garda region also produces familiar varietals.

6 Garda Bresciano

A collection of wines from the lower reaches of Lake Garda, including Gropello and the rounder Chiaretto from the Mincio valley.

7 San Martino della Battaglia

A tart white made from Tocai grapes of Friuli; there's also a dessert liqueur version.

8 Lugana

This balanced white is made from Trebbiano grapes on the southern shores of Lake Garda.

9 San Colombano

Milan's own red is chiefly significant for making the DOC level despite being grown on the outskirts of an industrial city.

10 Grappa

Italy's firewater is a *digestivo* ("digestive" liqueur) distilled from the leftovers of the grape-squeezing process.

Left **Villa Fiordaliso** Centre **Lake fish** Right **Barchetta interior**

Top 10 Restaurants

1 Ristorante Cracco, Milan

In 2000–2001, this bastion of fine Milanese cooking was completely overhauled and reopened under the guidance of Carlo Cracco, a pupil of Gualtiero Marchesi. With two Michelin stars, the menu is adventurous and the wine list exceptional. If the stratospheric prices make you cringe, know that around the corner is "Peck", also managed by Cracco, and one of the finest food emporia in Italy, where raw ingredients and prepared dishes can make up a glorious picnic *(see pp79 & 81)*.

Joia

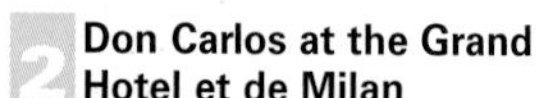

2 Don Carlos at the Grand Hotel et de Milan

Named after Verdi's opera, this restaurant offers a bold, impactful and highly memorable experience, serving Italian creative cuisine with oriental touches. The walls feature photographs and drawings of La Scala and the discreet background music is operatic. Open for dinner only, the kitchen closes at 11:30pm, which is late for Milan *(see p81)*.

3 Trattoria da Pino, Milan

Genuine Milanese home cooking is the order of the day here. You'll be squeezed in with the locals at this simple place but it's worth it for the delicious daily specials, bargain prices and great atmosphere *(see p81)*.

4 Joia, Milan

Swiss chef-owner Pietro Leeman spent time in the Orient before opening Milan's temple of vegetarian cuisine, and many of his dishes have a hint of the exotic that put them in a gourmet category. The wine list is joined by a selection of ciders and organic beers *(see p91)*.

5 Nicolin, Lecco

Located 3.5 km (2 miles) from Lecco, this restaurant has been run by the same family for over 30 years. The cuisine is traditional (ravioli stuffed with mushrooms and beef in barolo wine sauce with polenta) but also includes lake fish specialities, and the wine list is good. Tables on the lovely lakeside terrace are a draw during summer *(see p112)*.

6 Aimo e Nadia, Milan

Aimo and Nadia Moroni are acknowledged as being among the top chefs in all Milan. They are fanatical about hunting down the very best ingredients, and it shows in such delectables as risotto with pumpkin flowers and truffles. It's a bit of a haul from the centre of the city, but it is very much worth it *(see p97)*.

Villa Fiordaliso, Lake Garda

The setting is marvellous: beyond the historic Liberty-style villa (now a hotel) where D'Annunzio lived and Mussolini's mistress spent her final days, the tables are scattered about a shaded terrace lapped by lake waters. The cuisine is inventive and international, if sometimes overly minimalist *(see p122)*.

Il Sole di Ranco, Lake Maggiore

For more than 150 years, the Brovelli family has run an inn and *osteria* in the tiny lakeside village of Ranco. The restaurant – serving high-class creative cuisine and ancient recipes – has summertime seating on shaded terraces. The wine list offers more than 1,200 choices, and they'll set up a wine tasting to accompany your *degustazione* (tasting) menu *(see p102)*.

Barchetta, Lake Como

Restaurants in such touristy towns as Bellagio rarely rise to the level of quality that this has achieved under chef-owner Armando Valli and his assistant Davide Angelini. The signature dish is the *sinfonia degli otto sapori del lago*, a "symphony" of eight lake fishes. For dessert, try the traditional *paradel* – honey ice cream with raisins *(see p112)*.

Barchetta exterior

I Due Roccoli, Lake Iseo

Here, when the weather is fine, you can dine on the terracotta terrace high in the hills above Iseo, with a view across a rose-fringed lawn to forested mountains beyond. The cooking is superb, and makes wonderful use of lake fish and other fresh local ingredients *(see p129)*.

I Due Roccoli

Following pages **Lake Maggiore's Isola Superiore**

AROUND MILAN AND THE LAKES

Left **Dior shop window** Centre **Cova pastry shop** Right **Galleria Vittorio Emanuele II**

Milan's Historic Centre

THE CENTRO STORICO OF MILAN *is home to the cathedral, opera house, the magnificent royal palace, art-filled private mansions and busy pedestrian boulevards. This historic district was once the Roman city of Mediolanum, though its boundary walls vanished long ago. As well as historic sights, the area contains a grid of shopping streets around Via Montenapoleone known as the Quadrilatero d'Oro, or "Golden Rectangle". This small area is home to many major top-name designer boutiques as well as the head offices of all the biggest names in international fashion.*

Archi di Porta Nuova

Top 10 Sights

1. **Duomo**
2. **Palazzo Reale**
3. **Santa Maria presso San Satiro**
4. **Pinacoteca Ambrosiana**
5. **Palazzo della Ragione**
6. **Galleria Vittorio Emanuele II**
7. **San Fedele**
8. **La Scala**
9. **Museo Poldi-Pezzoli**
10. **Museo Bagatti Valsecchi**

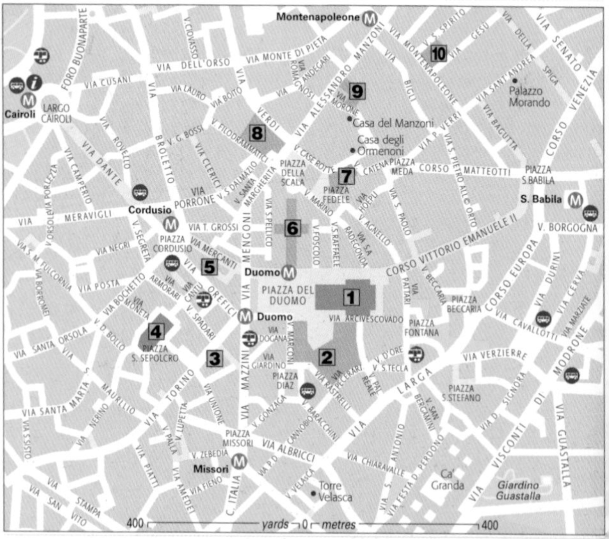

1 Duomo

The great travel writer H V Morton *(see also p51)* likened Milan's cathedral to a forest within the city, its thickets of columns and high vaulted ceilings providing the citizens with a spot of shade *(see pp10–11)*. ✆ *Map M4*

The Duomo – Milan's "forest"

2 Palazzo Reale

Once home to the Visconti and Sforza families, Milan's Neo-Classical Royal Palace was built under the aegis of Empress Maria Theresa in the 18th century and extended in 1939–56 with the Arengario, a towering pavilion on Piazza Duomo. This now houses the Museo del Novecento, an impressive collection of 20th-century paintings and sculpture. Palazzo Reale is also open for exhibitions. ✆ *Piazza del Duomo 12 • Map M4 • Museo del Novecento: see www.museodelnovecento.org*

3 Santa Maria presso San Satiro

Renaissance architect Bramante knew the only way to squeeze a Greek cross look into a space that only allowed room for a Latin cross was to concoct a layering of stuccoes, angled niches and frescoes behind the altar to give the illusion of a barrel-vaulted presbytery. Another notable feature is a *Pietà* group by Lombard sculptor Agostino De' Fondutis *(see also pp38–9)*. ✆ *Via Speronari 3 • Map L4 • 7:30–11:30am, 3:30–6:30pm Mon–Fri, 9am–noon, 3:30–7pm Sat & Sun • Free*

4 Pinacoteca Ambrosiana

Art-loving Cardinal Frederico Borromeo gave the city one of its greatest treasures when he bequeathed his private collection of works by Leonardo, Titian, Caravaggio and others, including the original cartoon for Raphael's famed *School of Athens (see pp18–19)*. ✆ *Map L4*

***Christ Among the Doctors*, Museo del Duomo, Palazzo Reale**

5 Palazzo della Ragione

Milan's 13th-century *broletto* (town hall) is a striking remnant of the Middle Ages *(see p36)*. ✆ *Piazza Mercanti • Map L4 • Open for exhibitions • Adm*

Left **San Fedele** Right **La Scala**

6 Galleria Vittorio Emanuele II

Before modern shopping centres and malls, there were *gallerie*. These late 19th-century high-class shopping arcades were roofed by the newest architectural technology of the age: steel-reinforced glass. Milan's Industrial Age-cum-Neo-Classical example connected Piazza del Duomo with La Scala and was so successful it spawned an Italy-wide trend, with copycat *gallerie* popping up in Naples, Genoa and Rome. *(See also pp36 & 56; 77–80 for shops.)* *Map M3*

7 San Fedele

The single nave construction of this 1559 Jesuit temple would become a blueprint for Lombard churches built in the Counter-Reformation. The Mannerist interior preserves some fine paintings, including Il Cerano's *Vision of St Ignatius*, Bernardino Campi's *Four Saints and Transfiguration*, and San Peterzano's *Pietà*. The sacristy is lined by 17th-century cabinets by the Jesuit Daniele Ferrari, who also carved the pulpit. *Piazza S Fedele • Map M3 • 7am–1:15pm, 4:30–6pm Mon–Fri • Free*

Milanese Luck

The central floor mosaic in the Galleria Vittorio Emanuele II sports the white-cross-on-red of the House of Savoy (representing Italy's newly crowned king who lent the gallery his name in 1868) and also a bull symbolizing Milan. According to local tradition, the Milanese ensure their good luck by stomping over the bull's testicles each time they pass.

8 La Scala

The world's greatest opera house was built in 1776–8 under the Austrians. It boasts a sumptuous interior, excellent acoustics and a staggering list of premieres *(see p51)*. Half destroyed in World War II, La Scala again became the toast of the town in 1946 when conductor Arturo Toscanini presided over its gala reopening. Check website for up-to-date programme listings and booking information. *Piazza della Scala • Map M3 • www.teatroallascala.org*

Galleria Vittorio Emanuele II

9 Museo Poldi-Pezzoli

One of the greatest private collections in Italy was bequeathed to the city by Gian Giacomo Poldi-Pezzoli in 1879. Its masterpieces all date from the last half of the 15th century, including works by Piero della Francesca, Bellini, Botticelli, Pollaiolo and Mantegna. There are some 18th-century Venetian cityscapes by Canaletto and Guardi, and the *Tapestry of the Hunt* from Tabriz is celebrated. There is also a collection of arms and armour, clocks and scientific instruments *(see also p40)*.

Via Manzoni 12 • Map M3 • 10am–6pm Wed–Mon (last adm 5:30pm) • Adm

10 Museo Bagatti Valsecchi

Two Milanese brothers created this Neo-Renaissance *palazzo* in 1883–94. They acquired as much as they could in the way of tapestries, furnishings and paintings from across Italy, and what they couldn't obtain in the original they hired an army of Lombard craftsmen to imitate. One room is copied from the ducal palace in Mantua, one from the Urbino's ducal seat, while another is lifted whole from a *palazzo* in Sondrio. The overall effect is a glorious mixture of Renaissance craftsmanship and Romantic sensibilities.

Via S Spirito 10/Via Gesù 5 • Map N3 • 1–5:45pm Tue–Sun • Adm

Museo Poldi-Pezzoli

A Day in Central Milan

Morning

Start at 10am amid the stupendous collections of **Pinacoteca Ambrosiana**.

Work your way south to Via Torino and the jewelbox of a church, **Santa Maria presso San Satiro** *(p73)*, then walk north up Via Torino until you reach the Piazza del Duomo, Milan's vast public living room.

Continue along the piazza's western edge and divert up Via Mercanti to see the raised porticoes of **Palazzo della Ragione**. Now cross the huge **Duomo** square to enjoy the marvels of Italy's second-largest cathedral *(pp10–11)*. Don't miss exploring its roof.

Take a platter of cheese and meats in **Zucca** *(p80)* at the entrance to **Galleria Vittorio Emanuele II**, the grandest shopping arcade in Italy.

Afternoon

Exit the arcade at Piazza della Scala, flanked by the famed opera house and **Palazzo Marino** *(p76)*. Behind the latter is the church of **San Fedele**. After seeing this walk northeast past the surreal **Casa degli Omenoni** *(p76)*.

Turn left to visit the excellent **Museo Poldi-Pezzoli**, then continue north on Via Manzoni, admiring its palazzi and Armani boutique, until you come to Milan's prime shopping street, **Via Montenapoleone** *(p57)*.

Shoppers will spend the rest of the day here; museum hounds can take in the **Museo Bagatti Valsecchi**. Both should stop for drinks at **Cova** *(p80)*.

Left **Piazza della Scala, near Palazzo Marino** Centre **Casa degli Omenoni** Right **Casa del Manzoni**

TOP 10 Best of the Rest

1 Ca' Granda

This massive complex – originally a hospital, now part of the University of Milan – took 400 years to complete *(see also p36)*. *Via Festa del Perdono 5 • Map M4–5 • 7:30am–7:30pm Mon–Fri, 8am–noon Sat • Free*

2 San Nazaro Maggiore

St Ambrose's fourth basilica was overhauled in the 16th century, when Bramantino added the Cappella Trivulzio. Lanino's *Martyrdom of St Catherine of Alexandria* is among its highlights. *Piazza S Nazaro in Brolo 5 • Map M5 • 7:30am–noon, 3:30–6:30pm Mon–Fri, 8am–12:20pm, 3:30–7pm Sat & Sun • Free*

3 Torre Velasca

This skyscraper is an oversized 1950s version of medieval tower design *(see p36)*. *Piazza Velasca 5 • Map M5 • No public access*

4 San Gottardo in Corte

Founded in 1336 as a chapel for the Palazzo Reale. *Via Pecorari 2 • Map M4 • 8am–noon, 2–6pm Mon–Fri, 2–4pm Sat, 8am–noon Sun • Free*

5 San Sepolcro

Built in 1030 on the site of the ancient Roman forum, this church preserves a long Romanesque crypt. *Piazza S Sepolcro • Map L4 • Noon–2pm Mon-Fri • Free*

6 Palazzo Marino

Milan's Mannerist town hall *(see p37)*. *Piazza della Scala/Piazza S Fedele • Map M3 • No public access*

7 Casa degli Omenoni

Sculptor Leone Leoni's 16th-century home has a magnificent façade flanked by a Liberty-style tower *(see also p37)*. *Via Omenoni 3 • Map M3 • No public access*

8 Casa del Manzoni

Manzoni, Italy's greatest 19th-century writer *(see p50)*, lived in this *palazzo*, now his museum. *Via Morone 1 • Map M3 • 02-8646-0403 • 9am–noon, 2–4pm Tue–Fri • Free*

9 The Palazzi of Via Manzoni

The boulevard from Piazza della Scala to Piazza Cavour has mansions from the 18th and 19th century: Brentani (No. 6), Anguissola (12), Poldi-Pezzoli *(see pp74–5)*, Gallarati Scotti (30) and Borromeo d'Adda (39–41). *Via Manzoni • Map M3–N2 • No public access*

10 Palazzo Morando – Costume Moda Immagine

In an elegant 18th-century townhouse, Milan's history is illustrated with paintings, artifacts and costumes. *Via Sant' Andrea 6 • Map N3 • 9am–1pm, 2–5:30pm Tue–Sun • Free*

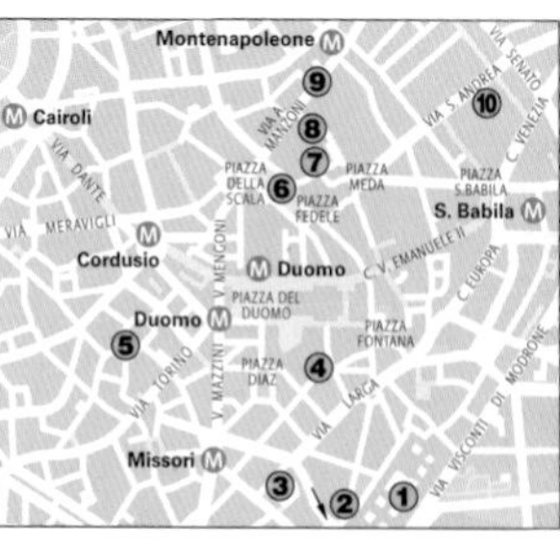

Left **Prada** Centre **Gianni Versace** Right **Gianfranco Ferré**

Top 10 Milanese Fashion Boutiques

1 Prada
Central outlets of the firm that transformed a handbag business into the high-fashion success story of the 1990s. *Galleria Vittorio Emanuele II & Via Montenapoleone 8 • Map M3*

2 Gianni Versace
Five floors mostly of menswear, with something for the ladies upstairs. Versace always manages to make surprises out of the ordinary. *Via Montenapoleone 2 (lower-price Versus label at Via San Pietro all'Orto) • Map N3*

3 Trussardi
Founded in 1911, this Bergamo glove-making firm is now one of the top designers of supple leather goods and ready-to-wear fashions. *Via Sant'Andrea 5 & Piazza della Scala 5 • Map N3*

4 Moschino
Everything from jeans to *prêt-à-porter* from the fashion iconoclast who died young in 1994. *Via Sant'Andrea 12 (also Via Durini 14) • Map N3*

5 Gianfranco Ferré
The former architect "built" each item of clothing around a woman to accentuate her natural beauty, a concept that remains a signature style of the label. *Via Sant'Andrea 15 • Map N3*

6 Missoni
Colourful knitwears from Ottavio and Rosita Missoni, who turned the fashion maxims of minimalism and basic black upside down. *Via Montenapoleone 8 (entrance Via Sant'Andrea) • Map N3*

7 Tom Ford
Synonymous with the resurrection of Gucci in the early 1990s, Tom Ford has gone from strength to strength. This luxury boutique is his first in Milan. *Via Verri 3 • Map M3*

8 Krizia
This Bergamo native delights in contrary fashions: colourful when black is in, miniskirts when conservative hem lines are the rage. *Via della Spiga 23 • Map N2*

9 Giorgio Armani
The first mega-department store devoted to just one fashion house – that of Milan's very own guru. *Via Manzoni 31 • Map M2*

10 Ermenegildo Zegna
Perfection in menswear is the watchword in this store with the best in fabrics and tailoring. *Via Montenapoleone 27 • Map M2*

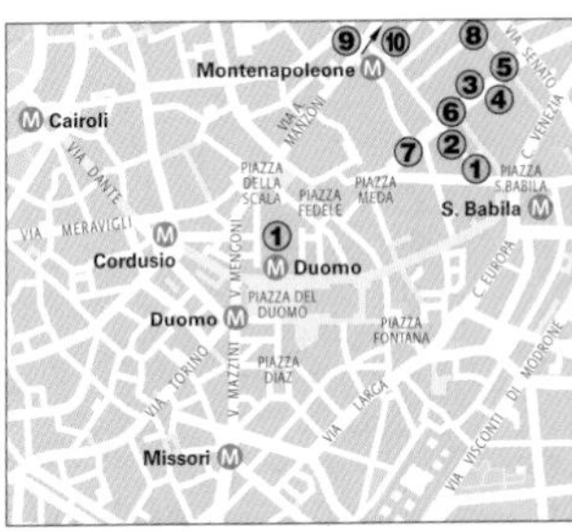

For more on Milan's top fashion designers **see p59**

Left **Ferragamo** Right **Valentino**

Top 10 Other Italian Designer Shops

1 Max Mara
After more than 50 years at the top of their class in women's wear, the Maramotti family's *prêt-à-porter* fashions are more vibrant than ever. *Corso Vittorio Emanuele II • Map N3*

2 Alessi
Tea kettles, silverware settings and other gorgeous items crafted by the top names in international industrial design. *Via Manzoni 14/16 • Map N3*

3 Ferragamo
Florentine cobbler Salvatore Ferragamo raised footwear to a modern art form when he shod Hollywood stars from Greta Garbo to Sophia Loren. Check out the sales in January and July. *Via Montenapoleone 3 (women's) and 20 (men's) • Map N3*

4 Mario Buccellati
Since 1919, no two Buccellatti jewels have been the same: each gemstone and silver filigree is hand-crafted by skilled artisans. *Via Montenapoleone 23 • Map N3*

5 Etro
Etro's trademark paisley and Pegasus icons abound on silk, cashmere and the finest wools. *Via Montenapoleone 5 (fragrances: Via Verri/corner Via Bigli) • Map N3*

6 Valentino
New York's Metropolitan Museum once mounted a show of Valentino's artistic clothing. Classy, chic and very desirable! *Via Montenapoleone 20 • Map N3*

7 Frette
Among the highest quality linens in all of Italy: drapes, pyjamas, sheets and pillows. *Via Montenapoeone 21 • Map N3*

8 Gucci
The mating "G"s that once decorated the leather goods of this firm, founded by a Florentine saddlemaker, are a thing of the past, but the quality is still topnotch. *Via Montenapoleone 5 (accessories & café: Galleria Vittorio Emanuele II) • Map N3*

9 Versace Home
Occupying half the block, this elegant store offers a tempting array of the Versace take on home furnishings. *Via Borgospesso 15A • Map M2*

10 Gio Moretti
This boutique offers Giovina Moretti's selection of the best of the season's top fashion. *Via della Spiga 4 (women's) and 26 (mens) • Map N2*

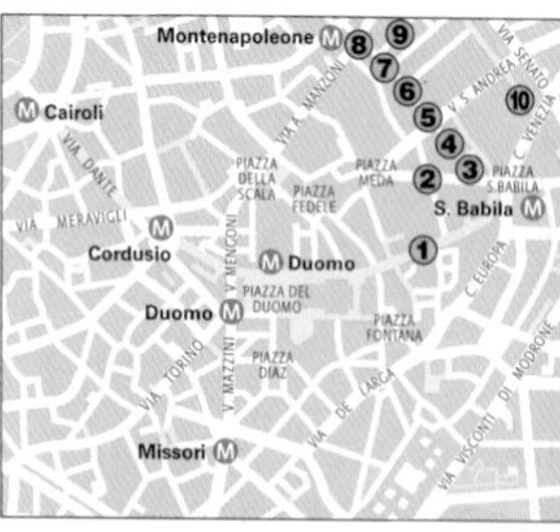

Left and Centre **Città del Sole** Right **Gastronomia Peck**

TOP 10 Other High-Class Shops

1 DoDo
This Milanese jeweller specializes in gold charms in the shape of animals and flowers, sold to support Italian wildlife. *La Rinascenete, Piazza Duomo • Map M4*

2 Cravatterie Nazionali
A vast selection of ties by Italy's top designers. *Via San Pietro all'Orto 17 • Map N3*

3 Mortarotti
Tired of boutique-hopping? Here's just one shop stocking a dozen major women's labels: Ferré, Missoni, Roberto Cavalli, Allegri, Eva Branca and more. *Via Manzoni 14 • Map M3*

4 Dmagazine
In the heart of high fashion sits a cut-price designer outlet, with Fendi scarves, Armani slacks, Prada sweaters and Helmut Lang suits among the items. Check in daily for bargains on the constantly rotating racks. *Via Montenapoleone 26 • Map N3*

5 Silbernagl
An eclectic mix of furnishings, porcelains, 19th- and 20th-century paintings, antique jewellery, Oriental vases and other items for decorating the well-heeled home. *Via Borgospesso 4 • Map M2*

6 Ricordi
Milan's huge subterranean branch of Italy's premiere chain of music and CD megastores, Ricordi has come a long way since it published the music of Rossini, Verdi, Bellini and Puccini. *Galleria Vittorio Emanuele II • Map M3*

7 Bocca
This long-time resident of the Galleria Vittorio Emanuele II is the place to find beautifully illustrated Italian exhibition catalogues, past and present, as a gift or for your own collection. *Galleria Vittorio Emanuele II • Map M3*

8 Città del Sole
This is Italy's main chain store for educational toys and games. *Via Orefici 13 • Map L4*

9 Gastronomia Peck
Superlative Milanese grocers since 1883, with three vast floors of meats, cheeses, vegetables, breads, wines and other delicacies. Its pricey restaurant is nearby *(see p81)*. *Via Spadari 9 • Map L4*

10 La Murrina
Central Milan's best shop for unique hand-made glass pieces. *Via Montenapoleone 18 • Map N3*

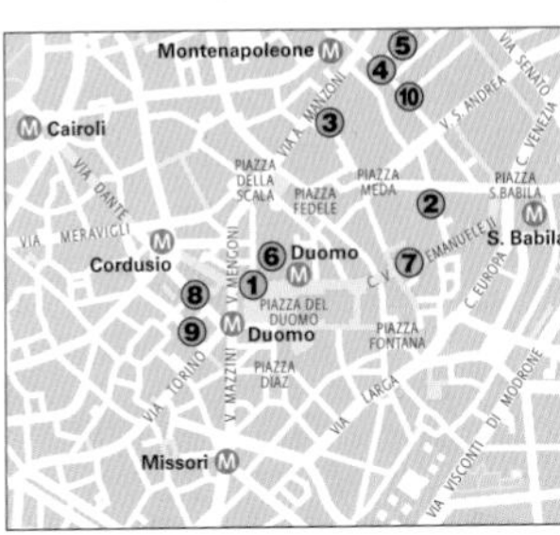

For more on Milan's shopping meccas and things to buy **see pp56–9**

Left **I Panini della Befi** Centre **Cova** Right **Caffè Martini**

Top 10 Venues, Clubs and Cafés

1 Zucca (Caffè Miani)
A gorgeous Liberty-style café, with views of the Duomo. Zucca was once owned by the Campari family of the apéritif fame *(see also p64)*. *Galleria Vittorio Emanuele II/Piazza Duomo 21 • Map M3 • www.caffemiani.it • €*

2 Caffè Martini
This café may be overpriced but is great for Duomo views and watching the people, processions and protest rallies at Milan's heart. *Via dei Mercanti 21 • Map L3 • €€*

3 Le Banque
This businessmen's lunch spot transforms into a yuppie disco – one of the few in Central Milan – with live music after 11pm; dress well. *Via Porrone 6 • Map L3 • 02-8699-6565 • www.lebanque.it*

4 Armani Privé
This classy nightclub has Japanese-inspired design and a strict door policy. Obligatory one drink minimum. *Via Pisoni • Map M3 • 02-6231-2655 • Closed Mon, Jun–Sep • €€*

5 Nepentha
Perennial Milan discotheque just one block south of the Duomo where the chic set come to dine and then dance the night away. *Piazza Diaz 1 • Map M4*

6 I Panini della Befi
Very popular *panino* bar at lunch, with umbrella-shaded tables on a pedestrian street. Stellar sandwiches, decent coffee. *Via Beccaria 4 • Map N4 • €*

7 Sant'Ambroeus
This historic café and tea room is also known for making some of the best chocolates in Italy *(see also p64)*. *Corso Matteotti 7 • Map N3 • €*

8 Cova
Nestling in the heart of Milan's boutique district since 1817, Cova offers excellent coffee and pastries *(see also p64)*. *Via Montenapoleone 8 • Map N3 • €*

9 Savini
This long-established eatery has a café and *pasticceria* as well as a fine restaurant. *Galleria Vittorio Emanuele II • Map M3 • 02-7200-3433 • €€€*

10 Sheraton Diana Garden
The mature, tree-shaded garden of the beautiful Sheraton Diana Majestic Hotel is the place to go for Happy Hour in summer. *Sheraton Diana Majestic Hotel, Viale Piave 42 • Map P1 • 02-2058-2081 • €*

For more entertainment venues in Milan see pp60–61

Price Categories

For a three-course meal for one with half a bottle of wine (or equivalent meal), taxes and extra charges.		
	€	under €20
	€€	€20–€30
	€€€	€30–€40
	€€€€	€40–€50
	€€€€€	over €50

Left **Luini** Right **Don Carlos at the Grand Hotel et de Milan**

Top 10 Places to Eat

1 Trattoria da Pino

Part of a dying breed, an *osteria* of butcher-paper place-mats and simple traditional dishes tucked into a room behind the street-front bar. *Via Cerva 14 • Map N4 • 02-7600-0532 • Lunch only • Closed Sun • No credit cards • €€*

2 Don Carlos at the Grand Hotel et de Milan

Open for dinner only, this restaurant is perfect for a post-opera meal. *(see also p68).* *Grand Hotel et de Milan, Via Manzoni 29 • Map M2 • 02-7231-4640 • Closed lunch & Aug • €€€€€*

3 Don Lisander

Creative regional, Tuscan and French cuisines in palatial surroundings. *Via Manzoni 12a • Map M2 • 02-7602-0130 • Closed Sun • €€€€€*

4 Trussardi alla Scala

Creative cuisine keyed on a small number of ingredients, a terrific wine list, red leather seats and views of Piazza della Scala make for a fine dining experience. *Piazza della Scala 5 • Map M3 • 02-8068-8264 • Closed Sun, Sat lunch • €€€€€*

5 Il Cantinone

Lombard–Tuscan hybrid in two classically elegant rooms. *Via Agnello 19 • Map M3 • 02-863-015 • Open daily • Closed 1 wk Aug • €€€€*

6 Luini

Luini may serve only *panzerotti* (pockets of stuffed dough), but locals flock here to eat them. *Via S Radegonda 16 • Map M3 • 02-8646-1917 • Closed Sun & Mon dinner • No credit cards • €*

7 Rinascente Top Floor Food Court

Great views and no fewer than seven options to choose from, including Obika, a Mozzarella bar. *Piazza del Duomo • Map M3 • 02-885-2471 • €€€*

8 Ristorante Cracco

Minimalist chic eatery complete with liveried doorman and astronomic prices *(see also p68).* *Via Victor Hugo 4 • Map L4 • 02-876-774 • Closed Sun, Aug & Christmas • €€€€€*

9 VUN

Fine dining in an elegant setting at the Park Hyatt Hotel. *(see p144).* *Via Tommaso Grossi 1 • Map L4 • 02-8821-1234 • Closed Sat lunch, Sun, 3 wks Aug • €€€€€*

10 Hostaria Borromei

Milanese and Italian dishes using fresh seasonal ingredients. *Via Borromei 4 • Map L4 • 02-8645-3760 • Closed Sat & Sun lunch • €€€*

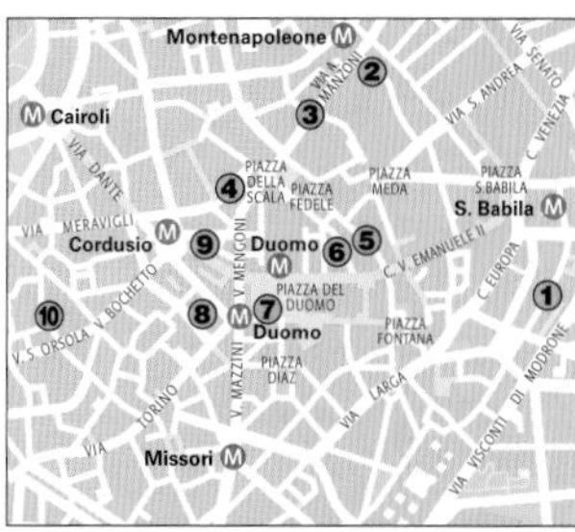

Note: *Unless otherwise stated, all restaurants accept credit cards and serve vegetarian meals*

Left **Museo di Storia Naturale** Centre **Museo dell'Ottocento** Right **Brek Restaurant**

Northern Milan

LEONARDO DA VINCI'S WORLD-FAMOUS *fading fresco, the city's best parks and several great museums form the highlights of this area. Three museums allow you to trace art from the medieval period (at the Castello Sforzesco) through the golden era of the Renaissance (at the Brera) to the challenges of Modernism (at the Villa Belgiojoso Bonaparte). A further two museums give an overview of Lombard history: ancient at the Museo Archeologico and that of the 19th century in the Risorgimento. Aside from the cultural hightlights, this part of town is also a great place for bargain shoppers, from warehouses lining the street south of the central railway station to the huge shopping boulevard of Corso Buenos Aires.*

TOP 10 Sights

1. Santa Maria delle Grazie
2. Civico Museo Archeologico
3. Castello Sforzesco
4. Parco Sempione
5. San Simpliciano
6. San Marco
7. Pinacoteca di Brera
8. Villa Belgiojoso Bonaparte – Galleria d'Arte Moderna
9. Cimitero Monumentale
10. Certosa di Garegnano

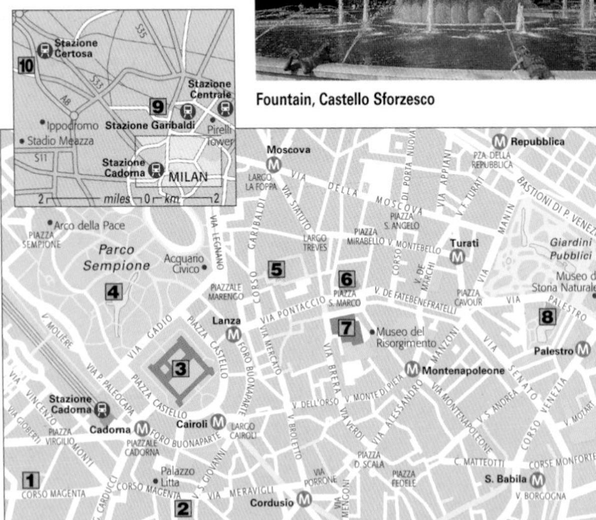

Fountain, Castello Sforzesco

Previous pages **Galleria Vittorio Emanuele II**

Santa Maria delle Grazie

1 Santa Maria delle Grazie

Leonardo's extraordinary fresco of the *Last Supper* adorns a wall of the convent refectory *(see pp8–9)* and is of course the chief attraction of this church. Other features include a magnificent Renaissance tribune, possibly designed by Bramante, who did the cloister and probably the main portal, too. *Piazza S Maria delle Grazie • Map J3 • Church 7am–noon, 3–7pm Mon–Sat, 7:30am–12:15pm, 3:30–8:15pm Sun • Free • For Last Supper viewings see p8*

2 Civico Museo Archeologico

A few pieces in an otherwise modest collection make this a worthwhile stop. The best are the Trivulzio Cup *(see p41)* and a stunning silver platter from the mid-4th century that displays in relief the deities of earth, sky, water and the zodiac – a resounding statement of faith in the old gods at a time of encroaching Christianity. There's also an exhibition devoted to urban planning and architecture in Milan from the 1st to the 4th century AD, which is located on the ground floor. In the 15th-century cloisters, half-demolished by bombs during World War II, are a pair of brick towers from the bastions of the Imperial-era city. *Corso Magenta 15 • Map K3 • 9am–1pm, 2–5:30pm Tue–Sun • Adm*

3 Castello Sforzesco

Milan's vast castle complex squats at the northwest corner of the historic centre, an intriguing combination of oversized courtyards, lithe towers and medieval nooks and crannies *(see pp16–17)*. *Map K2*

4 Parco Sempione

Milan's largest park started life as the 15th-century ducal gardens, though its layout, laced with pathways, dates from the late 19th century. A fine aquarium *(see p62)* is housed in a 1906 Liberty-style structure. There are also fountains (one by Giorgio de Chirico), exhibition halls, a sports arena and the triumphal Arco della Pace *(see p88)*. *Piazza Sempione • Map K2 • Park 6:30am–1 hour past sunset daily • Aquarium 9am–1pm, 2–5:30pm Tue–Sun • www.acquariocivicomilano.eu*

Castello Sforzesco

The Anaunia Martyrs

Three Byzantine missionaries, Sisino, Alessandro and Martirio (the name did not bode well), were sent by St Ambrose to Bishop Vigilio of Trent. Vigilio assigned them to convert pagans of the Trentino Alpine valleys. But locals of the Anaunia region were having none of it, and stoned the missionaries to death in 397, turning them into the region's first church martyrs.

5 San Simpliciano

One of four great basilicas built by St Ambrose in the 4th century (and finished by its namesake in 401) is popularly dedicated to the Anaunia Martyrs *(see box)*. The external walls are mostly original; the interior was renovated in the 11th and 12th centuries, and frescoed with a rainbow of angels and a *Coronation of the Virgin* by Bergognone in 1515. There are also patches of a late 14th-century fresco in a chapel off the choir. *Piazza S Simpliciano 7 • Map L2 • 9am–noon, 2:15–7pm Mon–Fri; 9:30am–7pm Sat & Sun • Free*

San Marco

6 San Marco

Of the original church, finished in 1254 and dedicated to Venice's patron St Mark as a tip of the hat for Venice's help in defeatir Barbarossa, all that remains main stone doorway, three in façade niches and the to the right bell tower. The res overhauled in the 19th cen with care to retain some 1 century frescoes. In the righ sept, there are earlier fresc dating to the 13th century, were rediscovered only in t 1950s. *Piazza S Marco 2 • Ma • 7am–noon, 4–7pm daily • Free*

7 Pinacoteca di Brera

In Northern Italy, Milan painting gallery is second c to Venice's Accade (though for sheer v the Brera wins). Si Napoleon inaugura the collection, it ha housed in the Jesu Palazzo di Brera. It' of the regions' mai 10, and for more o collection – which i cludes works by Pi della Francesca, Ra Bellini, Mantegna and Cara *(see pp12–15)*. *Map M2*

8 Villa Belgiojoso Bonaparte–Galleria d'Arte Moderna

Milan's Neo-Classical (1790 "Royal Villa" housed Napol in 1802 and Marshal Radetz until 1858. It is n an art gallery, wi works by Roman master Hayez; Neo-Classical sc Canova, whose b of Napoleon sits stairwell; Futuris Boccioni; and Tus pseudo-Impressi Macchiaioli, Lega Fattori. There are works by Moranc Corot, Gauguin,

Pinacoteca di Brera

Gogh and Picasso. The villa is set in lovely English-style gardens. *Via Palestro 16 • Map N2 • 9am–1pm, 2–5:30pm (last adm 5pm) Tue–Sun • Free*

9 Cimitero Monumentale

Milan's vast mid-19th-century cemetery is most popular for a pantheonic monument housing (among others) the remains of Alessandro Manzoni *(see p50)*. The grounds are filled with Art Nouveau tombs of Milan's top families – a free map shows where such notables as Arturo Toscanini rest in peace. Corners have been set aside for non-Catholic graves, and there's a monument to Jews deported by the Nazis. *Piazza Cimitero Monumentale • 8am–6pm (last adm 5:30pm) Tue–Sun • Free*

10 Certosa di Garegnano

The 14th-century Carthusian abbey has largely vanished under Milan's suburbs, but its church of Santa Maria Assunta survives. It has a fine late Renaissance façade, and the interior was frescoed by Daniele Crespi in 1629 with stories of the Carthusian order. *Via Garegnano 28 • 8am–noon, 3:30–5:30pm daily • Free*

Museo di Storia Naturale

Touring the Great Museums of Northern Milan

Morning

There are two major museums in this itinerary, so start off early at the **Castello Sforzesco** when it opens at 9am. Work your way up to **San Simpliciano** around 11am, then make your way southeast to the church of **San Marco**.

Continue up Via San Marco to have lunch at one of Milan's great simple trattorie, **Latteria San Marco** *(see p91)*, then head back down the street, cross Via Pontaccio, and plunge into the vast art collections of the **Pinacoteca di Brera**.

Afternoon

If you're an art fan, you'll probably spend the rest of the afternoon at the Pinacoteca, ready for a *passeggiata* and dinner when you emerge near closing time. But if it doesn't grab you, knock off after 90 minutes and you'll have time to continue east along Via Fatebenefratelli to Piazza Cavour.

From Piazza Cavour, go down Via Palestro to **Villa Belgiojoso Bonaparte**, then call in at the **Museo di Storia Naturale** *(p88)* to view dinosaur skeletons and wonderfully outdated 19th-century dioramas. Stroll over to Via Mozart to see how the sophisticated Milanese industrialist class lived at **Villa Necchi Campiglio** *(p88)* with its important art collections.

Finally, to round off a full and busy day, head for your dinner reservations at **Da Giacomo** *(p91)*.

Left **Pirelli Tower** Centre **Palazzo Litta** Right **Stadio Meazza**

TOP 10 Best of the Rest

1 Museo del Risorgimento

Find out about the heroes of Italy's 19th-century *risorgimento* (unification) movement at this museum. *Via Borgonuovo 23 • Map M2 • 9am–1pm, 2–5:30pm Tue–Sun • Adm*

2 Porta Nuova

Piecemeal city gate incorporating ancient Roman funerary reliefs and a 13th-century marble tabernacle. *Via Manzoni/Piazza Cavour • Map N2 • Free*

3 Villa Necchio Campiglio

An elegant 1930s villa with important paintings by masters such as Canaletto and Tiepolo *(see p37)*. *Via Mozart 14 • Map P3 • 10am–6pm Wed–Sun (last adm 5:30pm) • Adm*

4 Museo di Storia Naturale

Dinosaurs and taxidermied creatures are among the exhibits at the natural history museum founded in 1838. *Corso Venezia 55 • Map P2 • 9am–5:30pm Tue–Sun • Adm*

5 Palazzo Litta

Italy's state railway headquarters and a theatre occupy the expansive Rococo *palazzo* near the *Last Supper*. *Corso Magenta 24 • Map K3 • Open for exhibitions*

6 Museo Teatrale alla Scala

From hand-written scores to costumes, anything related to La Scala *(see p74)* can be found at this museum *(see also p41)*. *Largo Ghiringhelli 1 (Piazza Scala) • Map L/M3 • www.teatroallascala.org • 9am–noon, 1:30–5pm daily • Adm*

7 Arco della Pace

Luigi Cagnola built this magnificent triumphal arch in 1807 for Napoleon to pass through when visiting Milan. It didn't get finished quite in time and was inaugurated instead by a bemused Habsburg emperor. *Piazza Sempione • Map J1 • Free*

8 Pirelli Tower

Its reign as the world's tallest skyscraper lasted less than a decade, but this structure on the site of Pirelli's first tyre factory remains a symbol of Lombardy's robust economy *(see p37)*. *Piazza Duca d'Aosta • No public access*

9 Ippodromo

In 1999, Milan's horse track became home to a bronze horse cast by an American foundation determined to bring to fruition Leonardo da Vinci's oft-sketched equine tribute to Lodovico il Moro. *Via Piccolomini 2 • 9:30am–6pm*

10 San Siro (Stadio Meazza)

"The Scala of football", shared by rivals Inter and AC Milan. *Via Piccolomini 5 • Open for matches • Adm • Museum (Gate 14, Mon–Sat, adm)*

Left **Wine, Cotti** Right **Rufus**

Top 10 Shops

1 Emporio Isola

Discount outlet for noted clothing firms. Products are high quality and a wide range of styles, varying from elegant to pure chic, are available. Many bargains are on offer. *Via Prina 11*

2 Corso Como 10

While her sister served as editor of Italian *Vogue*, Carla Sozzani opened this boutique of expensive, eminently fashionable luxury labels on everything from clothes and accessories to books and kitchenware. There is also a café. *Corso Como 10*

3 Surplus

If you feel some fashions just never go out of style, visit Milan's top shop for second-hand and reproduction vintage couture from the past four decades. *Corso Garibaldi 7 • Map L1*

4 Cotti

Nearly 1,500 Italian wines, *grappas* (grape-based brandies) and other spirits are stuffed into this and gourmet foods shop, established in 1952. *Via Solferino 42 • Map L1 • www.enotecacotti.it*

5 Post-Design

Shop purveying the whimsical, stunning design objects produced by Milan's Memphis group, founded in 1981 by Ettore Sottsass and other young designers. *Via della Moscova 27 • Map L1*

6 Dolce e Gabbana

Housed in an old historical mansion, this men's apparel store includes a bar, barbers and grooming centre. *Corso Venezia 15 • Map P2*

7 Boggi

Boggi has been dressing the Milanese for years, providing them with classy clothing and footwear at reasonable prices. *Corso Buenos Aires 1 • Map P1*

8 Furla

Located towards the Porta Venezia end of this very long shopping street, Furla offers a constant flow of fashion-forward ideas in handbags. *Corso Buenos Aires/corner Via Omboni • Map P1*

9 Basement

This designer outlet is always worth a look with Gucci, Prada, Armani and other labels at extra-keen prices. *Via Senato 15 • Map N2*

10 Rufus

Discounts on designer shoes, with some top names coming in at under €90 a pair. *Via Vitruvio 35*

Left and right **Pasticceria Marchesi**

TOP 10 Cafés and Entertainment Venues

1 Bar Magenta
Comfortable, Parisian-style café with outdoor seating, a decent food menu, tasty cocktails and Guinness on tap *(see also p65).* *Via Carducci 13 at Via Magenta • Map K3 • €*

2 Pasticceria Marchesi
A delightfully Old World café and chocolatier near the *Last Supper (see also p65).* *Via Santa Maria alla Porta 11a • Map K3 • €*

3 Triennale DesignCafé
Masterminded by Carlo Cracco, whose eponymous restaurant has two Michelin stars, this café-restaurant in the Palazzo dell'Arte with splendid views of Parco Sempione is a great place for a light lunch. *Milan Triennale, Viale Alemagna • Map J2 • 02-8754-41 • Closed Mon • €€*

4 Just Cavalli Caffè
If you like Roberto Cavalli's in-your-face approach to fashion, you will love this lively café, with its leopard-skin patterned sofas. There is another Cavalli café in the store in Via della Spiga. *Between Via Shakespeare and Via Cameons, Parco Sempione • Map J2 • €€€*

5 Bar Bianco
A summer-only venue, this bar in the park is open till midnight, with the clientele switching from mothers and children to the city's trendiest out for dinner and cocktails. *Viale Ibsen, Parco Sempione • Map K2 • €€*

6 Bar Radetzky
This minimalist café has been around for many years, good for a quick espresso in the morning and an *aperitivo* in the evening. *Largo La Foppa 5 • Map L1 • €*

7 Alcatraz
Milan's biggest club staging top bands visiting Milan *(see also p61).* *Via Valtellina 21 • Map L1 • 02-6901-6352 • Closed Jun–Sep • €€€*

8 Hollywood
Fashion models and designers still hold on to Hollywood as their own club *(see also p61).* *Corso Como 15 • 02-659-8996*

9 Tunnel
This warehouse under the railway station sometimes features bands before they become famous. *Via Sammartini 30 • 336-135-8151*

10 Blue Note
This famous jazz club gives music lovers the opportunity to listen to the greatest jazz talents live *(see also p61).* *Via Borsieri 37 • Map M/N1 • 02-6901-6888 • Closed Mon (Oct–Mar), Jun–Aug • €€€€*

Price Categories

For a three-course meal for one with half a bottle of wine (or equivalent meal), taxes and extra charges.	
€	under €20
€€	€20–€30
€€€	€30–€40
€€€€	€40–€50
€€€€€	over €50

Left **Joia** Right **Sukrity**

TOP 10 Places to Eat

1 Pizzeria Grand'Italia

Enjoy a slice of some of the best pizza in town at this popular pizzaria. *Via Palermo 5 • Map L1 • 02-877-759 • €*

2 Latteria

This Brera district trattoria has become so famous you must line up early to enjoy the simple but well-prepared Milanese fare. *Via San Marco 24 • Map M1 • 02-659-7653 • Mon–Fri only • Closed Aug • No credit cards • €€€*

3 Da Giacomo

Superb fresh fish, grilled meats and traditional Milanese *cotoletta*, in an elegant Art Deco setting. Book ahead. *Via Sottocorno 6 • Map P3 • 02-7602-3313 • Closed 2 wks Aug, Christmas • €€€€€*

4 Joia

The Swiss chef at Milan's premier vegetarian restaurant creates brilliant meals even a sworn carnivore will love *(see also p68)*. *Via P Castaldi 18 • Map P1 • 02-204-9244 • Closed Sat lunch, Sun, Aug, Christmas • €€€€€*

5 Sukrity

Try one of Milan's oldest Indian restaurants for excellent-value tandoori and curries. *Via P Castaldi 22 • Map N1 • 02-201-315 • €€€*

6 Tipica Osteria Pugliese

Friendly place with simple, filling fare from Apulia in southern Italy. *Via Tadino 5 • Map P1 • 02-2952-2574 • Closed Sun • €€€*

7 Brek

Italian chain of fast-yet-excellent food. Carry your tray to the various food-prep islands, where dishes are cooked to order. *Piazzetta U. Giordano • Map N3 • 02-7602-3379 • €*

8 Trattoria Alla Cucina delle Langhe

Set in fashionable Corso Como, this long-established restaurant serves Piedmontese and Lombard classics on its main floor and more informal fare upstairs. *Corso Como 6 • Map L1 • 02-6554-279 • Closed Sun, 3 wks Aug • €€€€€*

9 Da Abele

Perfect for dinner if you love risotto, with three choices that change daily. Slightly off the beaten track and popular with locals. *Via Temperanza 5 • 02-261-3855 • Closed lunch & Mon • €€€*

10 Sakura Sushi Wok

Open every day, in a city where most places close at weekends, this large Japanese restaurant is useful to bear in mind. *Piazza XXV Aprile • Map M1 • 02-655-4604 • €€*

Note: *Unless otherwise stated, all restaurants accept credit cards and serve vegetarian meals*

Left **Bridge over Naviglio Grande** Centre **Rotonda della Besana** Right **Abbazia di Chiaravalle**

Southern Milan

THE CITY SOUTH OF THE CENTRO STORICO CORE *is dominated by the majority of Milan's most impressive churches: ancient Sant'Ambrogio and majestic San Lorenzo Maggiore; Sant'Eustorgio, with its remarkable carvings and paintings; the Renaissance piles of Santa Maria della Passione and Santa Maria presso San Celso; and the quirky 18th-century cloverleaf of La Besana. There's also the fantastic Science and Technology Museum, housed in a former convent; within its broad scope, the museum pays due homage to Leonardo da Vinci's oft-overlooked scientific genius with an excellent display of his technical drawings and models. Further to the south stretch the Navigli canals, once a bustling centre of Milanese commerce and now host to the city's liveliest nightlife and dining scene.*

TOP 10 Sights

1. Museo Nazionale della Scienza e della Tecnologia – Leonardo da Vinci
2. San'Ambrogio
3. San Lorenzo Maggiore
4. Museo Diocesano
5. Sant'Eustorgio
6. I Navigli
7. Santa Maria presso San Celso
8. Rotonda di Via Besana
9. Santa Maria della Passione
10. Abbazia di Chiaravalle

San Lorenzo

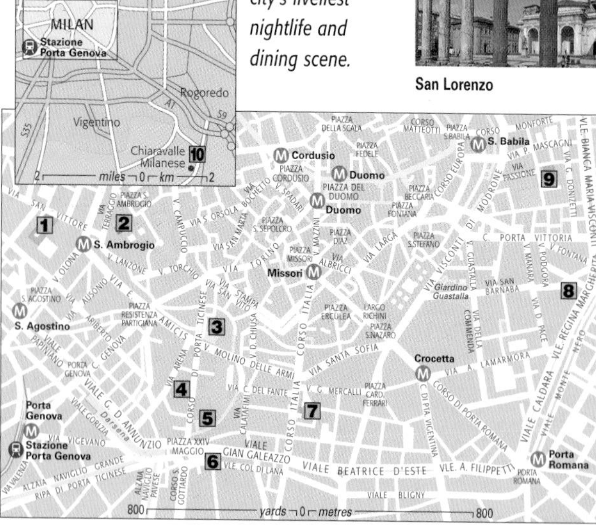

1 Museo Nazionale della Scienza e della Tecnologia – Leonardo da Vinci

The National Science and Technology museum knows what draws the crowds, hence its subtitle, "Leonardo da Vinci," which refers to the wooden scale models of his inventions, which fill the main hall. Also worth seeing are the telecommunications work of Marconi, displays on physics, cinematography and electricity and the Enrico Toti submarine *(see also p40).* *Via San Vittore 21 • Map J4 • www.museoscienza.org • 9:30am–4:30pm Tue–Fri, 9:30am–6pm Sat & Sun • Adm*

2 Sant'Ambrogio

Second only to the Duomo among Milan's great churches (and to many, rather more beautiful), this 4th-century basilica, with a cloistered entryway, Paleochristian mosaics, medieval carvings and late Renaissance frescoes, counts among the region's main Top 10 *(see pp20–21).* *Map K4*

3 San Lorenzo Maggiore

A free-standing row of 16 Corinthian columns – once part of a 2nd-century temple – sets San Lorenzo's frontal piazza off from the road. The vast interior of the church is magnificent and sombre. It was built on a circular plan, with a ring-shaped ambulatory and matroneum, or raised women's gallery, which often marked such early churches. The Chapel of S. Aquilino, to your right as you enter the building, preserves 4th-century mosaics, a 3rd-century sarcophagus and a Roman-era portal. *Corso di Porta Ticinese 39 • Map L5 • www.sanlorenzomaggiore.com • 7:30am–6:30pm Mon, Fri & Sat; 12:30–2:30pm Tue–Thu; 9am–7pm Sun • Free • Chapel: 9am–6:30pm daily; adm*

Sant'Ambrogio

4 Museo Diocesano

This museum houses important works from churches across Milan and Lombardy. In addition to numerous small panels by the 14th- and early 15th-century post-Giotto Gothic schools of central Italy, it holds 17th-century Flemish tapestries and some fine altarpieces. Among these are Hayez's glowing *Crucifixion with Mary Magdalene* and Tintoretto's *Christ and the Adulturer.* *Corso di Porta Ticinese 95 • Map K5 • www.museodiocesano.it • 10am–6pm Tue–Sun • Adm*

Cloisters of Sant'Ambrogio

5 Sant'Eustorgio

Sant'Eustorgio

The chapels opening off the right side of this ancient church were added between the 11th and 13th centuries, and frescoed in the 1300s and 1400s – Bergognone provided the triptych in the first one. The immense and impressive Arc of St Peter Martyr in the magnificent Portinari Chapel *(see p39)* was carved by Balducciο. *Piazza S Eustorgio • Map K6 • 7:30am–noon, 3:30–6:30pm daily. Museum: 10am–6pm • Free*

6 I Navigli

A city as grand as Milan needed a port, so in the 12th century, the Naviglio Grande – a 50-km/30-mile canal linking the city to Lake Maggiore – was created; the Naviglio Pavese (that connects Milan to Pavia) was added at the end of the 14th century. Today, the Navigli district is Milan's most lively, bohemian neighbourhood. Its old warehouses contain fashionable apartments and the towpaths are lined with restaurants, clubs, bars and shops. Its streets teem nightly with foodies out for a fine meal, young folks cruising the bars and street vendors spreading their wares. This part of the city stays open during the dog days of August. *South and east of Piazza XXIV Maggio • Map K6*

7 Santa Maria presso San Celso

The word *"presso"* reflecting its proximity to the abutting Romanesque church of San Celso, this Renaissance church shot up with remarkable speed between 1493 and 1506. Its most alluring aspect is the cloister-like court before the entrance, designed by Cesare Cesarino and considered one of the best examples of early 16th-century architecture in Milan. *Corso Italia 37 • Map L6 • 7am–noon & 4–6:30pm daily • Free*

8 Rotonda di Via Besana

Situated just south of Porta Vittoria, this Greek-cross church, dating from 1713, is now used for exhibitions. It is surrounded by a small green park bounded by a lovely rosette-shaped ring of a cloister. *Via Besana/Viale Regina Margherita • Map P5 • Open for exhibitions*

9 Santa Maria della Passione

Originally a modest Greek-cross church of 1486–1530, it was elongated with a massive nave and deep chapel niches in 1573 to make it the second largest church in Milan. Its interior is dominated by the work of Daniele Crespi: a portrait of San Carlo in the first chapel on the left, most of the Passion series below the cupola at

Rotonda di Via Besana

Canal Cruises

The tourist office sponsors twice-daily Navigli cruises (book ahead) with an audio CD to impart the history of these canals. On Saturdays this becomes a Cultural Excursion and on Sundays a Nature Tour, both ranging further afield with the aid of buses. All tours last roughly four hours. Browse www.naviglilombardi.it for more information.

the crossing and the organ doors. *Via Bellini 2 • Map P3 • 7:30am–noon, 3:30–6:15pm Mon–Fri; 9am–12:30pm, 3:30–6:30pm Sat & Sun • Free*

10 Abbazia di Chiaravalle

A countryside abbey now surrounded by the roar of suburban Milan, Chiaravalle has survived the centuries since its construction (between 1172 and 1221) remarkably well. Its lovely Romanesque architecture is enhanced by 15th- and 16th-century murals and a Luini *Madonna with Child* in the right transept. *Via S Arialdo 102 • 9am–noon, 2:30–5:30pm Tue–Sat; 2:30–5pm Sun • Free*

Abbazia di Chiaravalle

A Day with Leonardo

Morning

The influence of the Renaissance genius pervades the entire city of Milan.

Begin the day's itinerary at the Cordusio metro stop, then walk west on Via Meravigli three blocks to the corner with Via S Maria alla Porta for a cappuccino at **Pasticceria Marchesi**. Continue west, and pop into the **Museo Archeologico** *(p85)* for 20 minutes of historical musing.

Make reservations long in advance for an early admission to the *Last Supper (p85)*. Take time to fully appreciate Leonardo's art.

Go east along Corso Magenta to Via Carducci to relax at the Art Nouveau **Bar Magenta** *(see p90)* and enjoy an early lunch.

Afternoon/Evening

Turn down Via Carducci four long blocks to Via San Vittore (you'll see across the street the Pusterla di S Ambrogio, a remnant of the medieval city gates) and turn right for the **Museo della Scienza e della Tecnologia** *(p93)*.

At around 3:30pm double back along Via S Vittore to S Ambrogio. Trek down Via Edmondo De Amicis to Corso della Porta Ticinese, where your first stop is the magnificent **San Lorenzo Maggiore** *(p93)*. Peruse the works in the **Museo Diocesano**, then continue to **Sant'Eustorgio**.

A block south brings you into the bar and restaurant zone of the **Navigli**, ready for a post-itinerary drink and a meal *(pp96–7)*.

Left **Discount shopfront** Right **Porta Ticinese shoppers**

Top 10 Shops and Nightspots

1 Cavalli & Nastri
Vintage designer clothing for men and women, hand-picked for quality and condition. The favourite haunt of stylists and the stylish. Also at Via Brera 2. *Gian Giacomo Mora 12 • Map K5*

2 Floretta Coen Misul
Bargain-basement prices on brand-name clothing (Missoni, Ferrè, Yves St Laurent). Major label dresses under €150, suits under €200. *Via San Calocero 3 • Map J5*

3 Biffi
All the major labels for men and women, including whatever's hot this season, selected by Mrs Biffi. *Corso Genova 6 • Map J5*

4 El Brellin
A lively restaurant, Naviglio-front tavern and proud owner of a miniscule canal that was, in times gone by, used by Milanese washerwomen. *Vicolo dei Lavandai/Alzaia Naviglio Grande 14 • Map J6 • 02-5810-1351 • €€€€€*

5 Danese
Selling furniture icons of Italian industrial design from greats such as Bruno Munari and Enzo Mari, this is a must-visit shop for design enthusiasts. *Piazza San Nazaro in Brolo 5 • Closed Mon lunch, Sun, Aug • Map M5*

6 Scimmie
A veteran of Navigli nightlife – a jazz bar with regular live acts along with a restaurant and a barge for alfresco fun *(see also p60)*. *Via Asciano Sforza 49 • Map K6 • 02-8940-2874 • www.scimmie.it • €*

7 B-Fly
Located in one of the hippest streets in town, this is one of three Levi's Icon Stores worldwide. Buy select items from the Limited Editions of the Levi's Red, Levi's Vintage & Clothing and Levi's Blue lines. *Corso di Porta Ticinese 46 • Map K5*

8 Limelight
A post-modern disco owned by a group of Premier League footballers. The DJs spin everything from revival pop to salsa. *Via Castelbarco 11 • 346-033-8459 • €*

9 Il Salvagente
The best discount outlet in Milan, with two floors of clothing, shoes and bags at about 50% discount. Additional sales in January and June. *Via Fratelli Bronzetti 16*

10 Viale Papiniano Market
For designer bargains, head for Viale Papiniano with its many keenly priced stalls offering top brands. *Viale Papiniano • Map J5 • 9am–5pm Tue & Sat*

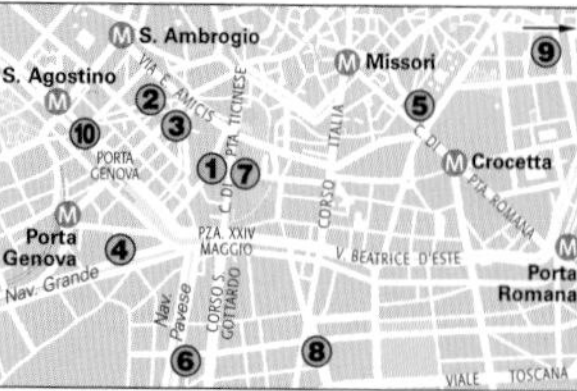

Price Categories
For a three-course meal for one with half a bottle of wine (or equivalent meal), taxes and extra charges.

€	under €20
€€	€20–€30
€€€	€30–€40
€€€€	€40–€50
€€€€€	over €50

Left **Premiata Pizzeria** Right **Trattoria Aurora**

TOP 10 Places to Eat

1 Ponte Rosso
Ignoring the hipness of Navilio, Ponte Rosso serves dishes from Milan and Trieste. *Ripa di Porta Ticinese 23 • Map J6 • 02-837-3132 • Closed Sun eve, 2 wks Aug • €€€€*

2 L'Ulmet
Traditional Milanese fare such as *ossobuco* (veal shank) is served in this friendly restaurant. *Via Olmetto 21 • Map L5 • 02-8645-2718 • Closed Sun, Mon lunch, Aug, Christmas • No vegetarian options • €€€€*

3 Le Vigne
A mix of local and Piedmontese cuisines. The *caramelle di ricotta e spinaci* is divine. *Ripa di Porta Ticinese 61 • Map J6 • 02-5811-3224 • Closed Sun, 2 wks Aug, Christmas • €€€*

4 Premiata Pizzeria
Navigli's most popular pizzeria, with semi-industrial decor and a terrace. *Via Alzaia Naviglio Grande 2 • Map K6 • 02-8940-0648 • Open daily • €*

5 Cantina della Vetra
Located in a verdant square, this restaurant serves risotto, ravioli and *ossobuco*. Good Sunday brunch. *Via Pio IV • Map K/L5 • 02-8940-3843 • Open daily • Closed I wk Aug, Christmas • €€€*

6 Cantina Piemontese
Small restaurant serving Piedmontese and Lombard fare. The vegetarian speciality is quiche with bean purée and artichokes. *Via Laghetto 2 • Map N4 • 02-7846-18 • Closed Sat, Sun, Aug • €€€*

7 Giulio Pane e Ojo
Bringing Roman brio to Milan, the food and atmosphere at this budget-priced trattoria are so popular that reservations are required at least five days in advance for dinner. *Via Muratori 10 • Map P6 • 02-5456-189 • Closed Sun • €€*

8 Sadler
Claudio Sadler, one of the top chefs in Milan, melds modern techniques with regional cuisine in a contemporary setting. *Via Ascanio Sforza 77 • 02-5810-4451 • Closed Sun, 1 wk Jan, 2 wks Aug • €€€€€*

9 Trattoria Aurora
Traditional restaurant with a long-established reputation. The vine-shaded setting is the restaurant's *pièce de resistence*. *Via Savona 23 • Map J5 • 02-8940-4978 • Closed Mon • €€€€*

10 Aimo e Nadia
Pricey and out in the suburbs, yet Aimo and Nadia (a Tuscan-born husband-and-wife team) run this place with exquisite taste throughout, and it ranks among Milan's very, very best *(see also p68)*. *Via R Montecuccoli 6 • 02-416-886 • Closed Sat lunch, Sun, 3 wks Aug • €€€€€*

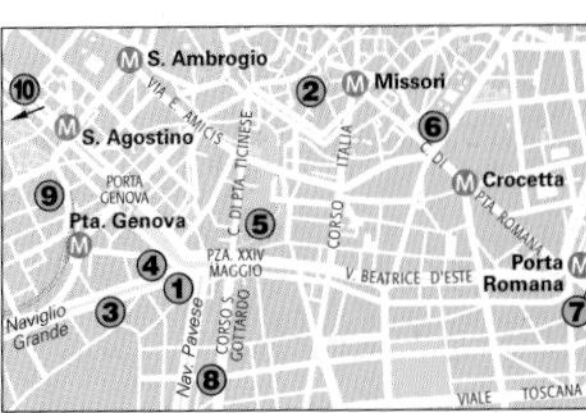

Note: *Unless otherwise stated, all restaurants accept credit cards and serve vegetarian meals*

Left **Isla Madre, Isole Borromee** Centre **Santa Caterina del Sasso** Right **Rocca di Angera**

Lake Maggiore

THE WESTERNMOST OF ITALY'S GREAT LAKES *straddles the Lombardy-Piedmont border and pokes its head into Switzerland. The southern half was, from the 15th century, a fiefdom of the powerful Borromeo clan. Maggiore's development as a holiday retreat for Europeans began in 1800 when Napoleon's Simplon highway from Geneva to Milan skirted its shores. Maggiore has fewer resorts than Garda and is not as breathtakingly pretty as Como. While the triplet Borromean Islands are stunning, few of Maggiore's other diversions can compare. Still, all this can play in Maggiore's favour if you're looking to avoid the over-development of Garda and the crowds of Como.*

Statue of Carlo Borromeo, Arona

TOP 10 Sights

1. Arona
2. Rocca di Angera
3. Stresa
4. Santa Caterina del Sasso
5. Isole Borromee
6. Verbania
7. Cannero Riviera
8. Cannobio
9. Ascona
10. Locarno

Stresa

1 Arona

This sprawling modern town was once a stronghold of the Borromeo family, but its fortress was razed by Napoleon. The only lasting monument to the great family is a disconcertingly enormous 17th-century bronze statue of San Carlo Borromeo. Clamber up a ladder-like stair to the head of the 23-m (75-ft) colossus to peek out through his pupils at the 17th-century church below. The road leading to this shrine was meant to be lined with 15 devotional chapels, but only two were finished. *Map A3 • Tourist info: Piazzale Duca d'Aosta • 0322-243-601*

Arona

2 Rocca di Angera

This medieval castle, a Borromeo fortress since 1449, preserves a hall of crude frescoes (1342–54), which count among the oldest surviving Lombard-Gothic works on a non-religious subject. Wooden staircases lead to the tower and lake views. Most of the rooms now house a Doll Museum, with its splendid collection of Japanese figures and 18th- and 19th-century European examples *(see also p42)*. *Angera • Map A3 • 0331-931-300 • end Mar–Oct: 9:30am–5:30pm daily • Adm*

3 Stresa

The gateway to the Isole Borromee *(see p100)* is a pretty lakeside town that offers hotels, a grid of trattoria-lined pedestrian streets and quite a good summer music festival *(see p52)*. Just south of town, the Villa Pallavicino has a botanical garden and small zoo. *Map A3 • Tourist info: 0323-301-50 • www.parcozoopallavicino.it*

4 Santa Caterina del Sasso

In thanks for being saved from a shipwreck in the 13th century, a local merchant built a chapel into the cliff face above the treacherous, deepest part of the lake. There are some frescoes, but the greatest attraction is the setting itself *(see also p42)*. *Outside Leggiuno • Map B3 • 8:30am–noon, 2:30–6pm daily (weekends only in winter) • Free*

Rocca di Angera

Left **Gardens, Isole Borromee** Right **Cannero Riviera**

5 Isole Borromee

From the 1650s to today, the trio of tiny islands in the middle of Lake Maggiore has drawn admirers for the gracious palaces and ornate gardens built by the Borromeo family, who still own everything but the fishing village on Isola Superiore. The islands are among Lombardy's top attractions *(see pp22–3)*. ✆ *Map A2/3*

6 Verbania

In 1939 Mussolini gave the ancient Roman name "Verbania" to a group of villages here that include little Suna, industrialized Intra and Pallanza, an important town in the Middle Ages. Pallanza's main sight is the landscaped garden of Villa Taranto *(see p44)*, while its Palazzo Viani-Dugnani houses a collection of landscape paintings. ✆ *Map A2 • Tourist info: Corso Zanitello 6–8 • 0323-556-669*

7 Cannero Riviera

Despite its northern locale, this sheltered promontory has a truly Mediterranean clime, enabling citrus trees and camellias to flourish. The lake vistas, steep medieval streets and 18th-century houses give it a pleasant feel. Most striking are the scraps of islands just offshore, sprouting glowering castles built by lake pirates in the 1400s *(see box)* and used by the Borromeo clan as a defensive line against the Swiss. ✆ *Map B2 • Tourist info: Via Angelo Orsi 1 • 0323-788-943*

The Bloody Mazzarditis

In the 15th century, the five Mazzarditi brothers built Cànnero's castle-islets as a base from which to rob villages and ships. The brothers kept any captured women chained inside, but murdered the men. In 1414, Cànnero sent 500 soldiers to attack the castle. Four brothers escaped, the fifth was drowned; his ghost is said to still haunt the ruins.

8 Cannobio

By the Swiss border at the base of a rushing mountain stream near the pretty Orrido di Santa

Cannobio

Anna gorge, Cannobio dates back more than 3,000 years, though its steep, crooked pebble lanes and old plastered buildings are mainly medieval. The harbour is filled with restaurant tables in summertime. *Map B2 • Tourist info: Via Antonio Giovanola 25 • 0323-71-212 • www.procannobio.it*

9 Ascona

Locarno's neighbouring town on the Swiss end of the lake has been a favourite haunt of such cultural giants as Kandinsky, Freud and Thomas Mann. It has a split personality: there's a Harley rally and Jazz festival in July, and a Rolls Royce gathering and classical music concerts in September. The streets are lined with top-end boutiques and sights such as the 16th-century church Santi Pietro e Paolo. Up on the mountainside is Monte Verità. From the late 1800s to the 1940s this was a utopian community that housed artists, vegetarians and nudists. *Map B2 • Tourist info: Via Papio 5 • 0041-917-910-091 • www.ascona-locarno.com*

10 Locarno

Sadly, most of this Swiss city at the northern end of the lake was rebuilt along modern Swiss lines of concrete, glass and steel. What remains of the medieval city, however, is worth crossing the border for. The 14th-century Castello Visconteo is a highlight, as is the Santuario della Madonna del Sasso (1497), which preserves paintings by Bramantino and Ciseri (avoid the long climb by taking the cable car). The Arps (20th-century artists Jean, Hans and Margherita) donated many works to a modern art gallery installed in the 17th-century Casa Rusca. *Map B1 • Tourist info: in the Casino on Piazza Grande • 0041-917-910-091*

A Day on Lake Maggiore

Morning

Be at the **Stresa** ferry dock *(see p99)* by 10am and buy a day pass for island hopping as well as admission tickets for the **Isole Borromee** sights.

Ride to **Isola Bella** first to spend two hours exploring the collections of the **Borromeo Palace** and the intricate gardens above it. Then catch the 12:25pm ferry for the short hop to the **Isola Superiore**, where you can settle into a lakeside table on **Verbano's** terrace for lunch with a view (book ahead of time, *see p102)*.

Mid-Afternoon

Wander the tourist/fishing village after lunch before continuing on the boat to **Isola Madre**.

The **Borromeo Villa** on Madre takes only a half hour to wander, but the vast botanical gardens surrounding it are a delight, thick with exotic flora and populated by colourful exotic birds. The multi-lingual map handed out explains many of the rare specimens and is remarkably informative too.

Try to catch a return ferry that stops on the mainland at Lido/Funivia for **Mottarone** – one stop before Stresa proper. Get off here and stroll along the little-used waterfront promenade for the final 20-minute walk back to downtown Stresa. You will be rewarded with a lovely late-afternoon view of the islands on your left, and romantically crumbling, abandoned villas on your right.

Price Categories

For a three-course meal for one with half a bottle of wine (or equivalent meal), taxes and extra charges.		
	€	under €20
	€€	€20–€30
	€€€	€30–€40
	€€€€	€40–€50
	€€€€€	over €50

Left **Osteria degli Amici** Right **Verbano**

TOP 10 Places to Eat

1 Osteria degli Amici, Stresa
This convivial spot has some outdoor tables and a menu ranging from pizza to freshly caught lake fish. *Via Bolongaro 31 • Map A3 • 0323-30-453 • Closed mid-Nov–early Feb • €€€*

2 Vecchio Tram, Stresa
On the hillside above Stresa and offering magnificent views of the lake, this restaurant serves alternative Mediterranean cuisine. Keyed on seasonal specialities, the menu changes monthly. *Via per Vedasco 20 • Map A3 • 0323-31-757 • Closed Nov–Feb: Mon–Thu • €€€€*

3 Piemontese, Stresa
Stresa's top restaurant piles on the elegance with bow-tied service and a wood-panelled dining room. What's best, though, is the vine-shaded cobbled court-yard, where you can enjoy hearty local dishes with a modern twist. *Via Mazzini 25 • Map A3 • 0323-30-235 • Closed Mon, Dec–Jan • €€€*

4 Verbano, Isola Superiore (Isola dei Pescatori)
The hotel's restaurant *(see entry 4, opposite)* is set on a terrace at the tip of the island, with great views. Regional dishes are very good and reasonably priced. *Map A3 • 0323-32-534 • Closed Nov–Mar • €€€€*

5 Milano, Verbania-Pallanza
Verbania's best restaurant serves classic Piedmontese dishes and lake fish in lovely grounds. *Corso Zanitello 2 • Map A2 • 0323-556-816 • Closed Tue & mid-Nov–Feb • €€€€€*

6 Boccon di Vino, Verbania-Suna
Laid-back little osteria serving home-made pastas and hearty seconds under vaulted ceilings. *Via Troubetzkoy 86 • Map A2 • 0323-504-039 • Closed Tue & Wed lunch in winter • €€*

7 Lo Scalo, Cannobio
The best of Cannobio's restaurants offers Piedmontese cooking with inventive touches. *Piazza Vittorio Emanuele II 32 • Map B2 • 0323-71-480 • Closed Wed in winter • €€€€€*

8 Il Sole, Ranco
A fresh take on Italian regional cuisine. Splendid view of lake from the terrace *(see p69)*. *Piazza Venezia 5 • Map A3 • 0331-976-507 • Closed Mon lunch, Tue lunch & mid-Nov–mid-Jan • €€€€€*

9 La Vecchia Arona, Arona
Franco Carrera is an enthusi-astic and innovative reinterpreter of "traditional" dishes. Book in advance. *Via Marconi 17 • Map A3 • 0322-242-469 • Closed Fri • €€€€*

10 Trattoria Campagna, Arona
A country trattoria in the hills above Arona, with a seasonal menu composed of excellent home-made pasta and lake fish. *Via Vergante 12 • Map A3 • 0322-57-294 • Closed Mon dinner (except Jul & Aug) & Tue • €€€*

***Note:** Unless otherwise stated, all restaurants accept credit cards and serve vegetarian dishes*

Price Categories

For a standard, double room per-night (with breakfast if included), taxes and extra charges.	
€	under €110
€€	€110–€160
€€€	€160–€210
€€€€	€210–€270
€€€€€	over €270

Left **Hotel Pironi** Right **Il Sole**

Top 10 Places to Stay

1 Grand Hôtel des Iles Borromées, Stresa

One of Italy's top hotels, with a starring role in Hemingway's *A Farewell to Arms (see p50)*, this is as sumptuous as you'd expect at the prices. ✆ *Corso Umberto I 67 • Map A3 • 0323-938-938 • www.borromees.it • €€€€€*

2 La Palma, Stresa

Almost luxury level living at relatively moderate prices: lake views from balconies, big marble bathrooms, pool. ✆ *Corso Umberto I 33 • Map A3 • 0323-32-401 • www.hlapalma.it • Closed Dec–Feb • €€€*

3 Primavera, Stresa

A small hotel in the pedestrian centre of Stresa. Simple rooms have the basic amenities. ✆ *Via Cavour 39 • Map A3 • 0323-31-286 • www.stresahotels.net • Closed winter (exc Christmas and New Year) • €*

4 Verbano, Isola Superiore (Isola dei Pescatori)

A lovely retreat. The much-requested rooms at the front overlook the restaurant *(see entry 4 on previous page)*. ✆ *Map A3 • 0323-30-408 • www.hotelverbano.it • Closed Nov–Mar • €€€*

5 Grand Hotel Majestic, Verbania-Pallanza

One of Maggiore's top hotels since 1870, with spacious rooms, grounds and spa. ✆ *Via Vittorio Veneto 32 • Map A2 • 0323-509-711 • www.grandhotelmajestic.it • Closed Oct–Mar • €€€€*

6 Hotel Pironi, Cannobio

The wedge-shaped 15th-century building has a frescoed loggia. Rooms exude antique charm. ✆ *Via Marconi 35 • Map B2 • 0323-70-624 • www.pironihotel.it • Closed mid-Nov–mid-Mar • €€*

7 Il Portico, Cannobio

Modern hotel in a quiet corner of town. Its porticoed restaurant and best rooms overlook the lake. ✆ *Piazza Santuario 2 • Map B2 • 0323-70-598 • No A/C • Closed Oct • www.hotelilportico.com • €*

8 Hotel Giardino, Ascona

Set in huge grounds overlooking the lake, yet within the city's residential area, this 72-room luxury hotel is a perfect urban oasis. Spa, indoor and outdoor pools and an 18-hole golf club can be found next door. ✆ *Via Segnale 10 • Map B1 • 0041-91-785-8888 • www.giardino.ch • €€€€*

9 Il Sole, Ranco

The best lodgings on the east shore. Rooms mix antique furnishings with modern comforts, and there's a great restaurant *(see entry 8 on previous page)*. ✆ *Piazza Venezia 5 • Map A3 • 0331-976-507 • www.ilsolediranco.it • Closed mid-Nov–Jan • €€€€*

10 Conca Azzurra, Ranco

A modern lakeside retreat with pool, tennis courts and spa. ✆ *Via Alberto 53 • Map A3 • 0331-976-526 • www.concazzurra.it • Closed Jan–mid-Feb • €€*

***Note:** Unless otherwise stated, all hotels accept credit cards and have air conditioning and en-suite bathrooms*

ALBERGO
GHISALLO

Left **Statue, Villa Melzi, Bellagio** Centre **Piazza del Duomo, Como** Right **Ferry, Tremezzo**

Lake Como

COMO IS THE BEAUTY QUEEN *of the Italian lakes, the turquoise and sapphire waters of its three arms – 50 km (30 miles) long, but rarely more than 2 km (1 mile) wide – backed by the snow-capped peaks of the pre-Alps. The area's diversity stretches from the windsurfers and alpine vistas in the north to the busy towns capping the southern arms, such as Como, a Roman town with a glorious cathedral and silk industry, and Lecco, full of literary associations with Manzoni's great novel* I Promessi Sposi. *For centuries Lake Como has seduced visitors and drawn in the wealthy to line its shores with gracious villas and verdant gardens; it has also inspired composers (Liszt, Verdi, Bellini) and writers such as Byron, Shelley and Wordsworth.*

Basilica di Sant'Abbondio

Top 10 Sights

1. **Duomo, Como**
2. **Basilica di Sant'Abbondio, Como**
3. **Brunate Funicular, Como**
4. **Villa Balbianello, Lenno**
5. **Villa Serbelloni, Bellagio**
6. **Villa Melzi, Bellagio**
7. **Villa Carlotta, Tremezzo**
8. **Villa Monastero, Varenna**
9. **Villa Cipressi, Varenna**
10. **Abbazia di Piona**

Caffe Rossi, Bellagio

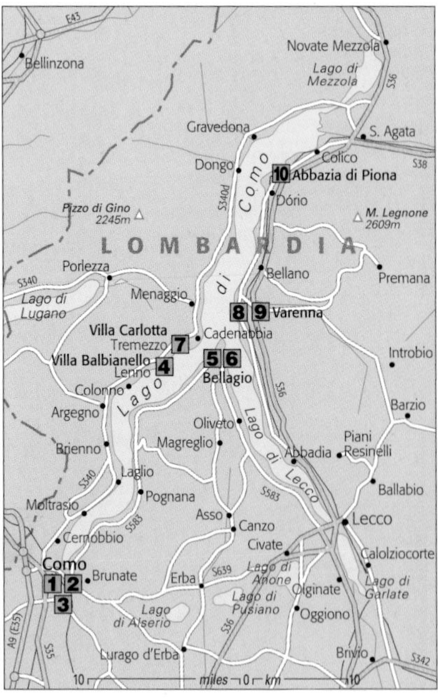

Previous pages **Bellagio on Lake Como**

Duomo, Como

1 Duomo, Como

Como's statue-clad cathedral was begun in 1396, but not capped with its Juvara-designed dome until 1740. On the façade, the pilasters are lined with saints and the main door is flanked by the seated figures of two local ancient scholars, Pliny the Elder and his nephew Pliny the Younger. The interior preserves an intricately carved and painted wooden altarpiece of 1492 and nine fabulous 16th-century tapestries, produced in Flemish, Florentine and Ferrarese workshops. *Piazza del Duomo • Map C3 • 031-265-244 • 7am–noon, 3–7pm • Free*

2 Basilica di Sant'Abbondio, Como

Standing forlorn in Como's industrial suburbs, this stony Romanesque church retains a pair of bell towers and an extended choir that links it, architecturally, to the Westwerk style of medieval Germany. The apse is gorgeously frescoed with a series of Biblical scenes. *Via Sant'Abbondio (off Viale Innocenzo XI) • Map C3 • 8am–6pm daily (to 4:30pm in winter) • Free*

3 Brunate Funicular, Como

The classic journey to this hillside village is to take a short walk from Como's harbour to the funicular station, then ride the funicular up to Brunate. You're rewarded with vistas over Como and the lake, and the starting point of many trails into the surrounding hills. *Piazza A De Gasperi • Map C3 • 031-303-608 • Every 15 mins 6am–10:30pm daily (to midnight daily in summer) • Adm*

4 Villa Balbianello, Lenno

The statue-lined balustrades fringed with flowers that outline the terraced gardens of this 1784 villa have caught the eye of many a film director. It is best to approach the villa by boat from Lenno and then proceed on foot. To tour the villa itself (pricey) you must book in advance. For more, *see p45. Lenno • Map C2 • 0344-56-110 • Mid-Mar–mid-Nov: 10am–6pm Thu–Tue • Adm*

Villa Balbianello

For places to stay around Lake Como **see p113**

Left **Bellagio's promontory** Right **Villa Melzi**

5 Villa Serbelloni, Bellagio

Bellagio's promontory has been prime real estate for millennia. Pliny the Younger had a villa named "Tragedy" here (it matched a "Comedy" home on the far shore), replaced by a castle in the Middle Ages, then a Stagna family villa in the 15th century. The last Stagna left it to his best friend Serbelloni in 1788. Serbelloni proceeded to rebuild the villa as a summer residence to the main house down in the village (now Grand Hotel Villa Serbelloni, *see p113*). In 1959, the summer home passed to the Rockefeller Foundation, and now visiting scholars can live and study here for short periods. It is not open to the public, but you can tour the gardens *(see p44)*. *Piazza della Chiesa, Bellagio • Map C2 • 031-951-555 • Tours mid-Mar–mid-Nov: 11am and 3:30pm Tue–Sun • Adm*

Villa Carlotta

Como Silk

Como has been Italy's silk capital since 1510. While they now import the spun thread from China, the fabrics Como's artisans weave is still the most sought-after by Milan's top designers. There are shops and warehouse stores all around town hawking silk wares. In the city outskirts there is even a Museum of Silk at Via Valleggio 3 (031-303-180; www.museosetacomo.com).

6 Villa Melzi, Bellagio

The meticulous gardens surrounding the Neo-Classical home of Francesco Melzi d'Eril, Napoleon's man in Italy, are now open to the public *(see also p44)*. *Lungolario Marconi • Map C2 • 031-950-204 • Apr–Oct: 9:30am–6:30pm daily • Adm*

7 Villa Carlotta, Tremezzo

One of the most sumptuous villas on the lake, with exquisitely landscaped gardens. Unusually, you can tour the art-strewn villa here, as well as its wonderful surrounds *(see also p44)*. *Tremezzo • Map C2 • 0344-40-405 • www.villacarlotta.it • mid-Mar–mid-Nov: 10am–4pm daily • Adm*

8 Villa Monastero, Varenna

This blissful villa – a former convent – has gardens that stretch right down to the banks of the lake, wonderfully shaded throughout by the canopies of

Villa Monastero

cypresses and palms *(see also p45)*. *Via Polvani 2 • Map C2 • www.villamonastero.eu • May–Sep: 9am–7pm daily • Adm*

9 Villa Cipressi, Varenna

The Cipressi villa has been altered throughout its 600-year life, though what you see today is largely 19th century. Its gardens are modest compared to others (including neighbour Villa Monastero) but, unlike most other villas on the lake, you can make this one your home – temporarily – since it's now a hotel *(see p113)*. For more, *see p45*. *Via IV Novembre 18 • Map C2 • 0341-830-113 • Mar–Oct: 9am–6pm daily • Adm*

10 Abbazia di Piona

At the tip of the Ogliasca peninsula sits this Benedictine abbey, cloaked in silence. The abbey was founded in the 9th century, and the little church has Romanesque carvings decorating the water stoups and the capitals and bases of the columns in the quiet cloister. The monks distil – and sell – some potent liqueurs too. *Signposted off the lake road • Map C2 • 0341-940-331 • 9am–noon, 2:30–5pm daily • Free*

Town Hopping

Morning

To cruise the lake you can buy point-to-point tickets, or peruse the single-ticket cruises that visit several towns and may include villa admissions. This itinerary assumes you have already checked out Como's sights before spending the night in **Bellagio**.

Begin the next day with a cappuccino at Bellagio's **Caffè Rossi** across from the dock before boarding the 10:30am boat to **Villa Carlotta**, where you have an hour to visit the collection of art and lush gardens of the lake's greatest villa.

Catch the ferry down to Isola Comacina to dig into a sumptuous feast at the **Locanda** *(see p112)*. After a second helping of their "spiked" coffee, you'll have a bit of time to work off the meal by exploring the island's overgrown church ruins before grabbing the boat back up the lake to **Varenna**.

Mid-afternoon

Continue walking off the big lunch by climbing up to the romantic, panoramic Castello di Vezio above town, then descend and pop into Varenna's little churches. Poke around the gardens of **Villa Monastero**, then finally head down to the lakefront arcade for a short stroll then a meal by the water at the splendid **Vecchia Varenna** *(see p112)*.

Unless you decide to spend a relaxing night in quiet and little visited Varenna, make sure you finish dinner before 9pm, when the last ferry leaves for Bellagio.

Left **Bellagio** Centre **Varenna** Right **Menaggio**

TOP 10 Lakeside Towns

1 Bellagio
A popular town, containing the gardens of villas Serbelloni and Melzi, a Romanesque church, a café-lined harbour front and a pretty warren of medieval alleys *(see p108)*. *Map C2 • Info at ferry dock on Piazza Mazzini • 031-950-204 • www.bellagiolakecomo.com*

2 Como
Italy's silk capital was founded by the Romans and has a spectacular cathedral *(see p107)*, a handful of modest museums, lots of boutiques and two ancient churches. *Map C3 • Tourist info: IAT, Piazza Cavour 17; 031-269-712; www.lakecomo.org • Local info: to the right of the Duomo; 031-264-215*

3 Varenna
Arguably, Varenna makes a better base for exploring the lake than crowded Bellagio. It has ferry links with major towns and everything from frescoed churches to lovely walks *(see pp108–9)*. *Map C2 • Info at Via IV Novembre 3 • 0341-830-367*

4 Menaggio
A pleasant little resort on the main ferry lines, with some modest Baroque churches. *Map C2 • Tourist info: Piazza Garibaldi 8 • 0344-32-924*

5 Tremezzo
A tiny resort whose main claim to fame is the Villa Carlotta *(see p108)*. *Map C2 • Tourist info: IAT, Via Regina 3; 0344-404-93*

6 Lecco
The capital of the lake's south-eastern arm is famous for sights linked to native writer Alessandro Manzoni, who set parts of his *I Promessi Sposi (see p50)* in the suburban hamlet of Olate. *Map D3 • Info at Via N Sauro 6 • 0341-295-720 • www.aptlecco.it*

7 Gravedona
The town has two fine medieval churches: Santa Maria del Tiglio and, up on the hillside, Santa Maria delle Grazie. *Map C2 • Info at Piazza Trieste • 0344-85-005*

8 Bellano
On Piazza S Giorgio sits the black-and-white striped façade of Santi Nazaro e Celso. A steep street leads to the entrance of the dramatic Orrido gorge. *Map C2 • Info at Via V Veneto 23 • 0341-295-720*

9 Lenno
Don't miss the 11th-century Santo Stefano and neighbouring baptistry. Just north of town, in Mezzegra, a black cross marks the spot where Mussolini was shot by partisans. *Map C2 • Info at town hall, Via S Stefano 7*

10 Civate
On tiny Lake Annone in the Brianza triangle between Como and Lecco, Civate is the access point to San Pietro al Monte, an 11th-century monastic complex. *Map D3 • Monastery: 346-306-6590; 9:30am–4pm Tue–Fri; 10am–noon, 1–3pm Sat; 9am–noon, 1:30–4pm Sun • Adm*

Browse **www.fromitaly.net/lakecomo** *and* **www.lakecomo.org** *for more information about Como's lakeside towns*

Left **Cycling** Centre **Windsurfing** Right **Divina Commedia**

Top 10 Things to Do

1 Playing a Round of Golf
If you have a handicap of 36 or less, try for a reservation at the Circolo Villa D'Este and check out the course of Golf Club Menaggio & Cadenabbia.
Circolo, Montorfano, 031-200-200 • Menaggio & Cadenabbia, 0344-32-103

2 Mountain Biking
The forested hills of Bellagio's peninsula make perfect mountain-bike country. Saddle up at a local hire shop. *Bike hire: Cavalcalario Club, Gallasco, 031-964-814, www.bellagio-mountains.it*

3 Windsurfing
The strong winds of the lake's northern end draw an international crowd of windsurfers.
Equipment hire: Windsurfcenter Domaso, 380-700-0010, www.wsc-domaso.com • Unione Sportiva Derviese, Dervio, 0341-804-159, www.usderviese.it

4 Horse Riding
Choose between English- or Western-style saddles and trek through mountain valleys off the Menaggio-Porlezza Road.
Trekking centre: Maneggio dei Tre Laghi, 392-032-2903

5 Climbing
Rock climb in the mountains ringing the lake's southeastern end. *Info at CAI, Via Papa Giovanni XXIII, Lecco, www.cai.lecco.it*

6 Kayaking
Get a different perspective on Como's fabled coastline, peeking into private lakeside gardens from a kayak or canoe.
Boat hire: Cavalcalario Club, Gallasco (see entry 2) *• Società Canottieri, Via Nullo 2, Lecco, 0341-364-273, www.canottieri.lecco.it*

7 Visiting the Divina Commedia, Bellagio
Theme pub with the top floor a cloud-frescoed "Paradise"; the ground floor "Purgatory"; and the tiny basement a papiermâché "Inferno". *Salita Mella 43–45 • 031-951-680 • www.divinacommedia.com*

8 Drinking at the Hemingway Pub, Como
It's debatable whether "Papa" actually drank atop the plush benches of this curious little bar tucked away near the port, but the cocktails are named after his books. *Via Juvara 16 • 031-271-631 • www.hemingway988.com*

9 Partying at Lido di Lenno, near Como
This typical Italian summertime venue is a beach with a bar serving snacks in the daytime, while on Friday and Saturday nights it becomes a club with DJs.
Map C2 • 0344-57093 • Closed Mon

10 Hanging out at Il Tana, Menaggio
Popular with the young crowd, this little bar in the piazza by the quay has live music on Fridays and Saturdays and DJ sets from 11pm. *Map C2 • Piazza IV Novembre • 0344-32558 • Closed Mon in winter*

Barchetta, Bellagio

Price Categories

For a three-course meal for one with half a bottle of wine (or equivalent meal), taxes and extra charges.	
€	under €20
€€	€20–€30
€€€	€30–€40
€€€€	€40–€50
€€€€€	over €50

TOP 10 Places to Eat

1 Sant'Anna 1907, Como
Creative local food is served at this traditional restaurant split into four elegant rooms. As well as meat or fish tasting menus there are some great vegetarian dishes. *Via Turati 3 • 031-505-266 • Closed Sat lunch, Sun • €€€€€*

2 Ristorante Sociale, Como
One of the best-value set menus on the lake draws a local post-theatre crowd, Como's soccer team and budget-minded travellers alike. *Via Rodari 6 • 031-264-042 • Closed Tue, Aug • €€€*

3 Barchetta, Bellagio
For such a beloved resort, Bellagio oddly lacks superlative eateries, save perhaps this "little boat". The recipes are local and well-prepared, the ambience amicable and the prices appropriate. *Salita Mella 13 • 031-951-389 • Closed Tue & Nov–Easter • €€€€*

4 Nicolin, Lecco
Garden seating, a homely atmosphere and gourmet set-priced menus make this a foodie haven in the village of Maggianico outside Lecco *(see also p68)*. *Via Ponchielli 54 • 0341-422-122 • Closed Sun dinner, Tue & Aug • €€€€*

5 Crotto dei Platani, Brienno
A mix of rustic and elegant at a restaurant set in the remains of a castle. Charming candlelit terrace tables and regional food prepared with an inventive touch. *Via Regina 73 • 031-814-038 • €€€€€*

6 Vecchia Varenna, Varenna
Housed in a 15th-century building, the most romantic restaurant on the lake offers a creative approach to local cuisine with an emphasis on lake fish. *Contrada Scoscesa 10 • 0341-830-793 • Closed Mon, Jan & Feb • €€€€*

7 Locanda dell'Isola Comacina, Ossuccio
This island eatery's fixed-price feast has remained unaltered since 1947: antipasto, trout, fried chicken, cheese, fruit, *gelato*, water, wine and brandy-spiked coffee. *Isola Comacina • 0344-55-083 • www.comacina.it/isola • No credit cards • Closed Nov–Feb, Tue in winter • €€€€€*

8 Pesa Vegia, Bellano
This small restaurant with a lakeside terrace specializes in lake and sea fish delicacies. Seasonal menu includes pan-fried *lavarello*. *Piazza Verdi 7 • 0341-810-306 • www.pesavegia.it • Closed Mon in winter • €€€*

9 Vecchia Menaggio, Menaggio
This homely trattoria is a favourite with locals for its fish and venison specials and its wood-fired pizzas. *Via al Lago 13 • 0344-32-082 • Closed Tue & Nov–Mar • €€€*

10 Trattoria S Stefano, Lenno
The place for outstanding lake fish and pasta. Fine views of the lake from the verandah. *Piazza XI Febbraio 3 • 0344-55-434 • Closed Mon & mid-Jan–mid-Feb • €€€*

***Note:** Unless otherwise stated, all restaurants accept credit cards and serve vegetarian meals*

Price Categories

For a standard, double room per night (with breakfast if included), taxes and extra charges.	
€	under €110
€€	€110–€160
€€€	€160–€210
€€€€	€210–€270
€€€€€	over €270

Left **Grand Hotel Menaggio** Right **Villa Cipressi, Varenna**

TOP 10 Places to Stay

1 Le Due Corti, Como
This ancient, rambling post house at the city's medieval walls has been a classy and atmospheric hotel since 1992. Excellent restaurant and popular bar, too. *Piazza Vittoria 12/13 • 031-328-111 • www.hotelduecorti.com • Closed mid-Dec–mid-Jan • €€€*

2 Hotel Terminus, Como
Set in lovely gardens, this former home of 19th-century Lombard aristocracy is full of atmosphere and lovely Art Nouveau details. *Lungo Lario Trieste 14 • 031-329-111 • www.albergoterminus.com • €€€*

3 Grand Hotel Villa Serbelloni, Bellagio
Bellagio's elegant summer villa was transformed into a hotel in 1873. Rooms are luxurious. Mini-apartments stay open year-round, as do the gym, beauty centre and indoor pool. *Via Roma 1 • 031-950-216 • www.villaserbe lloni.com • Closed Nov–Mar • €€€€€*

4 Du Lac, Bellagio
The friendliest family-run hotel in town happens to sit right on the lakeside piazza, with lovely views from charming rooms fitted with antiques. *Piazza Mazzini 32 • 031-950-320 • www.bellagiohoteldulac.com • Closed Nov–Easter • €€€*

5 Suisse, Bellagio
Ten simple rooms with TVs and fancy wood furniture above a restaurant. *Piazza Mazzini 8/10 • 031-951-755 • www.hotelsuissebellagio.com • Closed Jan–Feb • No A/C • €€*

6 Villa d'Este, Cernobbio
This sumptuous Renaissance villa is consistently rated among the top 10 hotels in the world and has long attracted royalty and celebrity. No expense is spared (antiques and silk, marble and mahogany), as is reflected in the bill. *Cernobbio • 031-3481 • www.villadeste.it • Closed mid-Dec–Feb • €€€€€*

7 Milano, Varenna
Beloved old family-run *pensione*. There are ceiling fans throughout. *Via XX Settembre 35 • 0341-830-298 • www.varenna.net • Closed Nov–Mar • €€*

8 Villa Cipressi, Varenna
Rooms in this 16th-century villa *(see p109)* are spacious, with killer views – remarkable for the price. *Via IV Novembre 18 • 0341-830-113 • www.hotelvillacipressi.it • Limited A/C • Closed Nov–Mar • €€*

9 Grand Hotel Menaggio
This 19th-century villa retains a Belle Époque air, but rooms are modern. *Via IV Novembre 93 • 0344-30-640 • www.grandhotelmenaggio.com • Closed Nov–Mar • €€€€*

10 Grand Hotel Tremezzo
The gardens of this 1910 hotel rival those of neighbouring Villa Carlotta. The opulence extends to the highly impressive rooms. *Via Regina 8 • 0344-42-491 • www.grandhoteltremezzo.com • Closed Nov–Mar • €€€€€*

***Note:** Unless otherwise stated, all hotels accept credit cards and have A/C (air conditioning) and en-suite bathrooms*

Left **Il Vittoriale, Gardone Riviera** Centre **Torri del Benaco** Right **The road to Castello di Arco**

Lake Garda

GARDA IS THE MOST SPORTING *of the Italian lakes. The crosswinds to the north and the dominating slopes of Monte Baldo draw windsurfers and paragliders, while other adrenaline-filled sports, such as rock climbing, and the more leisurely pursuit of golf, provide further distractions. Garda also enjoys some of the best Roman-era remains in northern Italy at Sirmione and Desenzano, as well as atmospheric medieval castles in Torri del Benaco, Malcesine, Valeggio and Sirmione. Since the 18th century, Garda's summer villas and verdant gardens have lured such luminaries as Goethe, Byron and D H Lawrence, though the region also found infamy as the place of Mussolini's last stand.*

Botanico Hruska, Gardone Riviera

TOP 10 Sights

1. Giardino Sigurtà
2. Gardaland
3. Grotte di Catullo, Sirmione
4. Rocca Scaligera, Sirmione
5. Villa Romana, Desenzano
6. Isola del Garda
7. Il Vittoriale, Gardone Riviera
8. Giardino Botanico Hruska, Gardone Riviera
9. Torri del Benaco
10. Castello di Arco, near Riva

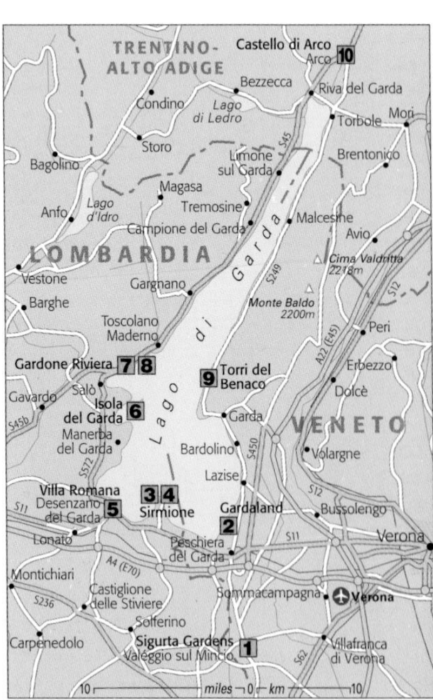

Giardino Sigurtà

1 Giardino Sigurtà

Carlo Sigurtà spent 40 years irrigating and planting this barren hillside in order to turn it into one of Italy's great gardens, with manicured lawns and pathways amid vibrant flower beds and reflecting pools. Hidden along the far western edge are some large enclosures where deer and goats run free. The gardens are a 20-minute drive south of the lakeside. *Via Cavour 1, Valeggio • Map G5 • 045-637-1033 • www.sigurta.it • Mar–Nov: 9am–6pm daily • Adm*

2 Gardaland

Under the icon of a goofy green dragon named Prezzemolo ("Parsley"), the park boasts roller coasters and carnival rides, a water park, jungle safari, ice shows, dolphin tricks and medieval spectacles. Italy's greatest theme park isn't quite Disneyland, but it's a hoot for the kids. *On the shore road, north of Peschiera • Map G4 • 045-644-9777 • www.gardaland.it • Closed Nov–Mar (except Christmas–New Year) • Adm*

3 Grotte di Catullo, Sirmione

Though the ancient Roman poet Catullus did take his holidays at Sirmione, there's no evidence to suggest that this vast, ancient house at the very tip of Sirmione's peninsula was actually his villa – in fact, it was probably built after Catullus's death, sometime in the 1st century BC. It is the best surviving example of a Roman private home in northern Italy, but this didn't stop it being misnamed a "grotto", the result of the romantically overgrown and cave-like state it had assumed by the Middle Ages. *Via Catullo • Map G4 • 030-916-157 • 8:30am–7pm Tue–Sun (to noon Sun; to 4:30pm in winter) • Adm*

4 Rocca Scaligera, Sirmione

The 13th-century keep is at the narrowest point of Sirmione's long, thin peninsula. The striking, angular pale grey stone citadel, in use as a fortress until the 19th century, still dominates and protects the town – the only way to enter Sirmione is over the moat on one of the castle drawbridges, then under one of its squat gate towers. It's worth climbing the 30-m (95-ft) tower for the grand panorama. *Piazza Castello • Map G4 • 030-916-468 • 8:30am–7pm Tue–Sun • Adm*

Gardaland entrance

Il Vittoriale, Gardone Riviera

5 Villa Romana, Desenzano

The most important late Imperial villa remaining in Northern Italy was built in the 1st century BC, but the excellent polychrome floor mosaics are mostly of the 4th and 5th centuries. By that time, the local Romans were Christianized, which explains the late 4th-century glass bowl engraved with an image of Christ. *Via Crocefisso 2 • Map G4 • 030-914 3547 • 8:30am–7pm Tue–Sun (to 5pm mid-Oct–Feb) • Adm*

6 Isola del Garda

Garda's largest island once supported a monastery that attracted the great medieval saints: Francis of Assisi, Anthony of Padua and Bernardino of Siena. The monastery was destroyed by Napoleon and replaced in 1890–1903 with a Neo-Gothic Venetian-style villa and luxuriant gardens. Two-hour guided tours are available and, though expensive, do include a boat ride and a snack. *Boats from Barbarano and San Felice • Map G4 • 328-384-9226 • www.isoladelgarda.com • May–6 Oct: Tue & Thu at 9:40am • Adm (book in advance)*

7 Il Vittoriale, Gardone Riviera

This over-the-top villa was built by poet, solider and adventurer Gabriele d'Annunzio, one of Italy's most flamboyant characters from the turn of the 20th century *(see p45)*. *Map G4 • 0365-296-511 • www.vittoriale.it • Apr–Sep: 9:30am–7pm (last adm 6pm) Tue–Sun; Oct–Mar: 9am–1pm, 2–5pm Tue–Sun • Adm*

8 Giardino Botanico Hruska, Gardone Riviera

This small but lovely set of botanical gardens features more than 2,000 species on a terraced hillside *(see p45)*. *Gardone Riviera • Tourist info: IAT Gardone; 0365-203-47 • 15 Mar–15 Oct: 9am–6pm daily • Adm*

9 Torri del Benaco

This little town was once the capital of Lake Garda and important enough in the 14th century for Verona's Scaligeri family (who controlled much of Lake Garda) to build one of their castles. This one contains a modest museum on local history including the prehistoric rock carvings found on the

Giardino Botanico Hruska

Castello di Arco

nearby mountainsides. To see some of these 8,000-year-old etchings, follow signs off the main road up to Crer then walk up the trail for about 15 minutes to a spot where the rock face shows through the undergrowth. *Map G4 • Castle: Viale Fratelli Lavanda 2; 045-629-6111 • mid-Jun–mid-Sep: 9:30am–1pm, 4:30–7:30pm; mid-Sep–Oct & Apr–mid-Jun: 9:30am–12:30pm, 2:30–6pm • Adm*

10 Castello di Arco, near Riva

Perched above town, this 12th-century castle is in a state of near-total ruin. Only one wall remains of the central keep, and the sole room in the complex to survive intact was filled with debris until 1986. When it was cleared, several excellent late 14th-century frescoes were found, depicting nobles playing at board games and war. *Map H2 • 0464-510-156 • Apr–Sep: 10am–7pm; Mar & Oct: 10am–5pm; Nov–Feb 10am–4pm daily (last adm 1 hr before closing) • Adm*

Lakeside Battles

In the 13th–15th centuries Venice vied with Milan for control of Lombardy *(see p32)*. The town of Torbole *(p120)* at the northern end of Lake Garda was the scene of a historic Milanese victory in 1439. Venice was caught while trying to smuggle supplies to the besieged town of Brescia – 26 ships had been sailed up the Adige River and dragged overland via Torbole into the lake when discovered.

Two Days on Lake Garda

Day One

If you're here to relax and sightsee rather than thrash the waves up near **Riva** *(see p120)*, then spend your days on the southern end of the lake. **Sirmione** *(p120)* is both a charming and lively base.

On your first day, stop in **Desenzano** *(p120)* to see the **Villa Romana** before driving out to Sirmione itself. Walk out to the far tip of the peninsula to wander the ruins of the **Grotte di Catullo** *(p117)*. On your way back into town, divert to the right to pop into San Pietro and see its medieval frescoes.

Navigate the throngs of the tiny centre to clamber up the balustrades of the **Rocca Scagliera** *(p117)* for a sunset panorama.

Take a *passeggiata* (stroll) with the crowds before heading down to the **Il Girasole** *(p122)* for an exquisite evening meal.

Day Two

On day two, drive around to **Gardone Riviera** *(p120)* to tour Gabriele d'Annunzio's delightfully idiosyncratic **Il Vittoriale**, then have a refined meal on the terrace of the **Villa Fiordaliso** *(p122)*.

After lunch, take the time to wander the grounds at **Giardino Botanico Hruska** before either making your leisurely way back to Sirmione – if you are basing yourself there – or heading further up the lake to explore the small lakeside towns of **Limone** or **Riva** *(p120)*.

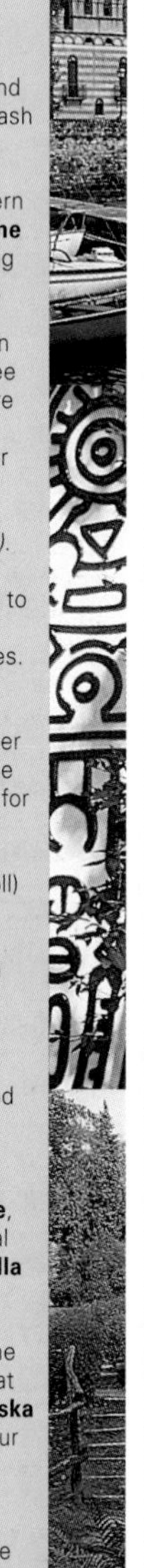

Left **Riva del Garda** Centre **Malcesine** Right **Torbole**

Top 10 Lakeside Towns

1 Sirmione
The loveliest town on the lake is set at the tip of a long peninsula. It has the ruins of an ancient Roman villa and a remarkably intact medieval castle *(see p117)*. *Map G4 • Tourist info: Viale Marconi 8 (just before town entrance) • 030-916-114 • www.comune.sirmione.bs.it*

2 Desenzano
A large and delightful town, settled in the Bronze Age and a retreat since the Roman era. Its top attraction is the Villa Romana *(see p118)*. *Map G4 • Tourist info: Via Porto Vecchio 34 • 030-374-8726*

3 Salò
This genteely faded resort became the capital of Mussolini's short-lived Republic of Salò (1943–5) in the closing chapters of World War II. *Map G4 • Tourist info: Piazza San Antonio 4 • 0365-21-423*

4 Gardone Riviera
The fruits of Gardone's long popularity as a resort developed into magnificent villas and gardens, including the Giardino Botanico Hruska and Gabriele d'Annunzio's Il Vittoriale *(see p118)*. *Map G4 • Tourist info: Corso Repubblica 8 • 0365-20-347*

5 Toscolano–Maderno
These twin towns enjoy a great beach and the glorious church of Sant'Andrea, with its Romanesque capitals and fading frescoes. *Map G4 • Tourist info: Via Sacerdoti, Maderno • 0365-641-330*

6 Limone sul Garda
Limone is tucked in a cove, with a long beach, small harbour and dozens of hotels, most of which are closed from November until Easter. *Map G3 • Tourist info: Via Sacerdoti, Maderno • 0365-546-083 • www.limone.com*

7 Riva del Garda
A bustling town, blessed with good sailing and the medieval Torre d'Apponale and Rocca Castle. Just inland lies Arco, home to a ruined castle *(see p119)*. *Map H3 • Tourist info: Largo Medaglie d'Oro 5 • 0464-554-444 • www.gardatrentinonline.it*

8 Torbole
History put Torbole on the map in 1439 *(see box on p119)*. Aside from that, the town is known chiefly as a good base for windsurfing. *Map H3 • Tourist info: Via Lungolago Verona 19 • 0464-505-177*

9 Malcesine
Among exhibitions on local natural history and prehistory, the town's castle contains a room devoted to Goethe, who was briefly suspected of being a spy when seen sketching the castle. *Map H3 • Open in high season • Tourist info: Via Gardesana 238 • 0457-400-044*

10 Bardolino
Bardolino has been famous since Roman times for its light red wine. The town also has two wonderful Romanesque churches. *Map G4 • Tourist info: P Aldo Moro • 045-721-0078*

Browse **www.provincia.brescia.it, www.gardatrentinonline.it** *and* **www.garda.com** *for more about Garda's lakeside towns*

Left **Windsurfing** Centre **Lakeside swimming** Right **Rock climbing**

TOP 10 Things to Do

1 Windsurfing

Each summer, windsurfers from across Europe descend on Garda's wind-pounded northern shores – especially in Riva and Torbole – for some of the best lake surfing on the continent. Surf hire shops can be found in Riva, Torbole and Sirmione.

2 Diving

While this isn't the tropics, the waters are clearer than you might expect. Subterranean surprises include an underwater Jesus near Riva. Equipment is available in various outlets.

3 Mountain-Biking

Whether you want to explore the flatlands to the south, tackle mountains rising sheer from the north shores, or simply wend along the lake itself, hire a bike to see Garda at a leisurely pace.

4 Climbing and Paragliding

For adventure sports such as climbing and canyoning, head to Arco, just north of Riva, for the Guide Alpine or Multi Sport Centre for a paragliding run, or the Paragliding Club in Malcesine. *Guide Alpine, Arco, 0464-507-075, www.guidealpinearco.com • Multi Sport Centre, Arco, 0464-543-269, www.multisport3.com • Paragliding Club, Malcesine, 366-594-4289*

5 A Round of Golf

The golf at Garda isn't great, but if you want to break out the nine-iron, there are courses on the southwest shore and one on the east shore. *Garda Golf, Soiano del Lago, 0365-674-707 • Golf Bogliaco, Toscolano, 0365-643-006 • Ca' degli Ulivi, Marciaga di Costermano, 045-627-9030*

6 Fura Club, Lonato

One of the best clubs in Italy, Fura is a visual experience – a screen surrounds the dance floor, so you can watch yourself dance. *Via Lavagnone 13 • Map G4 • 030-913-0652 • www.fura.it*

7 Caffè Casino, Arco

Open all day and evening, with a pretty glass- and iron-covered dining terrace and lots of live music events. *Via Delle Palme 6 • Map H3 • 0464-512-874 • Wed–Mon*

8 Caffè Grand Italia, Sirmione

Long-established *gelateria* with an impressive list of sundaes. *Piazza Carducci • Map G4 • 030-916-006 • Closed Nov–Mar*

9 Golden Beach, Desenzano

This stylish beach club in Desenzano del Garda offers an idyllic setting in which to enjoy a lakeside drink. There's also a buffet restaurant. *Via Zamboni 7 • Map G4 • 339-368-6845*

10 CocoBeach, Lido di Lonato

This sophisticated locale has a disco, restaurant and beach club with stunning lakeside view. *Via Catullo 5, Lido di Lonato • Map G4 • 349-581-0205 • Coco Club open Fri, Sat & Sun evenings • Closed Oct–Apr*

Price Categories

For a three-course meal for one with half a bottle of wine (or equivalent meal), taxes and extra charges.	
€	under €20
€€	€20–€30
€€€	€30–€40
€€€€	€40–€50
€€€€€	over €50

Left **Antica Hostaria Cavallino** Right **Gemma**

Top 10 Places to Eat

1 Esplanade, Desenzano

Stupendous lake views and a perfect balance of creative cuisine and traditional recipes. Delicious local cheeses and 1,500 wines in the cellar. *Via Lario 3 • Map G4 • 030-914-3361 • Closed Wed • €€€€€*

2 Antica Hostaria Cavallino, Desenzano

This restaurant offers local dishes and freshly caught lake fish, along with an exceptional wine list. *Via Gherla 30 • Map G4 • 030-912-0217 • Closed Mon, Sun eve & Nov • €€€€€*

3 Villa Fiordaliso, Gardone Riviera

A gorgeous Art Nouveau villa and hotel *(see also p123)*, serving impeccable food that revisits the formidable tradition of Italian cooking *(see also p69)*. *Via Zanardelli 150 • Map G4 • 0365-20-158 • Closed Mon & Nov–Feb • €€€€€*

4 Il Girasole, Sirmione

An elegant restaurant in the historic centre serving Italian food with an innovative twist. In summer you can eat alfresco on the flower-filled terrace. *Via Vittorio Emanuele 72 • Map G4 • 030-919-182 • Closed Jan–Mar • €€€€€*

5 La Rucola, Sirmione

The Bignotti family's genteel restaurant offers a creative menu based on seasonal ingredients and local fish and meats. *Via Strentelle 3 • Map G4 • 030-916-326 • Closed Thu, Jan • €€€€€*

6 Vecchia Malcesine, Malcesine

Up on the panoramic terrace overlooking the town, you can enjoy lake specialities and cool breezes. *Via Pisort 6 • Map H3 • 045-740-0469 • Closed Wed & Nov–Feb • €€€€€*

7 Gemma, Limone

A charming, family-run place with a waterside terrace. Lake fish, organic meats and truffles all feature on the menu. *Piazza Garibaldi 12 • Map G3 • 0365-954-014 • Closed Dec–Feb • €€€€*

8 Birreria Maffei, Riva

Riva's Tyrolean roots show in this "Austrian" *Bierhalle*, where *wurstel* (sausage) and tasty *schnitzels* hold sway on the menu. *Via Maffei 7 • Map H3 • 0464-553-670 • Closed Dec–Feb • €€*

9 Bella Napoli, Riva

A Sicilian couple has run this crowded joint for more than 30 years, but they stick to a tried and tested Neapolitan recipe for their wood-oven pizzas. *Via Diaz 29 • Map H3 • 0464-552-139 • Closed Wed, mid-Nov–early Mar • €€*

10 Gardesana, Torri del Benaco

Book ahead for a table on this palace's long terrace overlooking the harbour. A highly praised mix of regional and international cooking. *Piazza Calderini 5 • Map G4 • 045-722-5411 • Closed lunch, dinner Mon, Nov–Feb • €€€€*

***Note:** Unless otherwise stated, all restaurants accept credit cards and serve vegetarian meals*

Price Categories

For a standard, double room per night (with breakfast if included), taxes and extra charges.

€	under €110
€€	€110–€160
€€€	€160–€210
€€€€	€210–€270
€€€€€	over €270

Left **Grand Hotel Fasano** Right **Sole**

TOP 10 Places to Stay

1 Park Hotel, Desenzano

A modest hotel with classic decor and rooms overlooking the water. *Lungolago Cesare Battisti 17 • Map G4 • 030-914-3494 • www.parkhotelonline.it • €€€*

2 Villa Fiordaliso, Gardone Riviera

Five rooms including the suite where Mussolini and his mistress hid in their last weeks. Lakeside terrace for dining *(see also pp69 & 122)*. *Corso Zanardelli 150 • Map G4 • 0365-20-158 • www.villafiordaliso.it • €€€€€*

3 Grand Hotel Fasano, Gardone Riviera

A Grand Dame of a hotel, spread along a lakeside garden of palms and willows. For extra privacy, ask for a room in Villa Principe, a former hunting lodge. *Corso Zanardelli 190 • Map G4 • 0365-290-220 • www.ghf.it • Closed Oct–Easter • Amex, Diners not accepted • €€€€€*

4 Park Hotel Villa Cortine, Sirmione

An exclusive Neo-Palladian stunner sitting on a panoramic perch above its own regal gardens and beach. Antique furnishings and exquisite dining. *Via Grotte 6 • Map G4 • 030-990-5890 • www.palacehotelvillacortine.com • Closed late Oct–Easter • €€€€€*

5 Grifone, Sirmione

A delightful budget hotel that is fairly quiet and right on the lake with easy access to the beach. *Via Bocchio 4 • Map G4 • 030-916-014 • No A/C • €*

6 Sole, Riva del Garda

One of the best hotels in Riva: lakeside piazza location; great value pizzeria; and free bicycles for guests. *Piazza 3 Novembre 35 • Map H3 • 0464-552-686 • www.hotelsole.net • Closed Dec–Feb (open for Christmas) • €*

7 Hotel Du Lac et Du Parc, Riva del Garda

A luxurious retreat, with a fitness and beauty centre, a small park with tiny lakes, pools and a tennis court. Access to the gorgeous sandy beach. *Viale Rovereto 44 • Map H3 • 0464-566-600 • www.dulacetduparc.com • Closed Nov–Mar • €€€€€*

8 Le Palme, Limone sul Garda

Venetian-style rooms, most overlooking the lake, and a small pool in gardens that are shaded by palm trees. *Via Porto 36 • Map G3 • 0365-954-681 • www.sunhotels.it • Closed Nov–Easter • €*

9 Malcesine Hotel, Malcesine

The town's oldest hotel sits on the little port square – ask for a room overlooking the water. The low prices also include half-board. *Piazza Pallone 4 • Map H3 • 045-740-0173 • No A/C • Closed Nov–Mar • €€*

10 Romantik Hotel Laurin, Salò

A 1905 villa with exquisite detailing, spacious high-ceilinged frescoed rooms and a tiny garden pool. *Viale Landi 9 • Map G4 • 0365-220-22 • www.laurinhotelsalo.com • €€€*

***Note:** Unless otherwise stated, all hotels accept credit cards and have A/C (air conditioning) and en-suite bathrooms*

Left **Piazza del Comune, Cremona** Centre **Isola San Giulio, Orta** Right **Leoncino Rosso, Mantua**

Smaller Lakes and Towns

WHILE IT IS TRUE THAT THE LAKES OF Maggiore, Como and Garda are the best-developed and most obvious tourist destinations of the region, offering a wide range of accommodation and watersports facilities, do not overlook the lesser-known lakes and towns of Lombardy. The museums of Bergamo, Mantua and others may not be as important as Milan's, the villas less grand than Como's, but a few days spent off the beaten path can offer a rewarding break from the crowds that throng Milan's great sights and back up traffic for hours along the big three lakes.

Top 10 Sights

1. Lake Orta
2. Lake Varese
3. Lake Lugano
4. Bergamo
5. Lake Iseo
6. Lake Idro
7. Brescia
8. Mantua
9. Sabbioneta
10. Cremona

Mantova

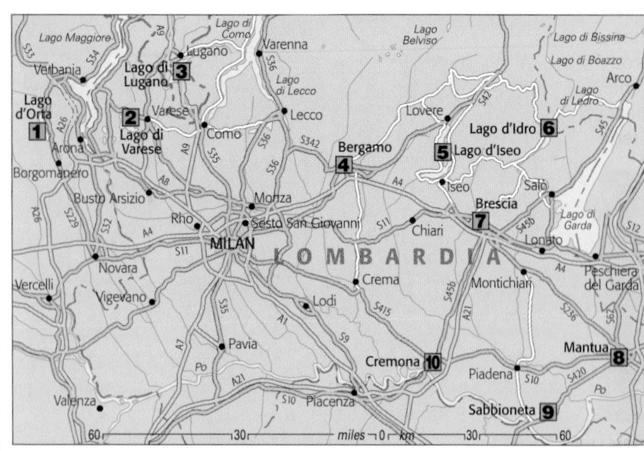

1 Lake Orta

Great at all times of the year, this is the region's westernmost lake situated at the foothills of the Alps. Its main town – with a traffic-free, medieval centre – is Orta San Giulio. Above the town, some 20 minutes on foot, is the Sacro Monte. On this wooded hillside are 20 chapels featuring sculptures depicting the life of Saint Francis of Assisi. Boats sail from Orta to the tiny idyll of Isola San Giulio. At the north end of Lake Orta, Omegna is an important centre of Italian industrial design, and is home to the firms of Alessi and Bialetti *(see also p58)*. The Forum Museum celebrates this utilitarian art form. *Map A3 • Tourist info: Via Panoramica in Orta S Giulio, 0322-905-614; www.distrettolaghi.it • Forum Museum: Omegna; www.forumomegna.org; adm*

2 Lake Varese

Varese is part of a quartet of small lakes (along with Monate, Comábbio and pond-sized Biandronno) that were popular with 18th-century Lombard landscape painters for their bucolic settings, Romanesque churches, mirror-like waters and Alpine backdrops. A few factories notwithstanding, the area is largely unchanged today. Roads rarely touch the lake shores, forcing detours into lakeside villages. This marshy region has yielded some important prehistoric finds, most especially on Lake Varese's Isolino islet (catch a boat from Biandronno, June–September), though the actual finds are kept at the Musei Civici in Varese town. *Map B3 • Tourist info: Via Romagnosi 9, Varese • 0332-281-913*

Lake Lugano

3 Lake Lugano

Lake Lugano snakes between Italy and Switzerland, and its principal resort, Campione d'Italia, is in fact an Italian enclave within Switzerland's borders. Campione is a slightly raucous island of pizza restaurants and gambling casinos interrupting the more staid Swiss shoreline, where to the south, outside Melide, is the delightfully kitsch Swiss Miniatur, with its vaguely accurate "map" of Switzerland, including all its major monuments reproduced at 1/25 of their actual size. *Map B2–C2 • Tourist info: Campione d'Italia, Via Volta 3; www.campioneitalia.com • Swiss Miniatur, Nr Melide; www.swissminiatur.ch; adm*

Lake Varese

Piazza Vecchia, Bergamo

4 Bergamo

A vibrant city of medieval streets, fashionable boutiques and Renaissance churches, Bergamo is one of the Top 10 of the region *(see pp26–7)*. *Map D3*

5 Lake Iseo

This is the prettiest of the smaller lakes, and the town of Iseo itself – with modest hotel complexes and watersports facilities – is as touristy as it gets. Further north, at Lovere, Galleria Tadini has a small collection of paintings by the likes of Jacopo Bellini, Tintoretto and Tiepolo. The interior of the church of Santa Maria della Neve, on the edge of Pisogne, is another delight, its abundant frescoes painted by Romanino in 1532–4 (if the church is locked, enquire at the café inside the adjacent cloisters). *Map E3–4 • Tourist info: IAT Lungolago Marconi 2, Iseo; 030-980-209; www.lagodiseo.org • Galleria Tadini, Lovere; Map F3; May–Sep: daily; Oct–Apr: Sat, Sun & hols; adm*

6 Lake Idro

This slip of a lake just west of Garda is renowned for its trout, sailing, windsurfing and skiing in the surrounding mountains. Sports and the lake's natural beauty are to the fore, while cultural highlights are Anfo's 16th-century castle and the 15th-century frescos in the church of Sant'Antonio. *Map G3 • Tourist info: Via Trento 16, Idro; 0365-83-224*

7 Brescia

The industrialized face of Brescia hides a fine medieval and Renaissance centre, with several mementos of its time as a Roman colony (including a temple and theatre). In the ancient San Salvatore e Santa Giulia monastery is the excellent Museo di Santa Giulia, a repository of prehistoric, Roman and medieval objects and artworks. The painting gallery (Pinacoteca Tosio-Martinengo) has works by local Renaissance artists and the great Raphael and Tintoretto. *Map F4 • Tourist info: Via Musei 32; 030-374-9916; www.provincia.brescia.it • Museo di Santa Giulia, Via dei Musei 81; 030-297-7834; Tue–Sun; adm*

8 Mantua

The palaces, churches and artworks by Mantegna and Giulio Romano help make Mantua, too, one of the entire region's Top 10 *(see pp28–9)*. *Map H6*

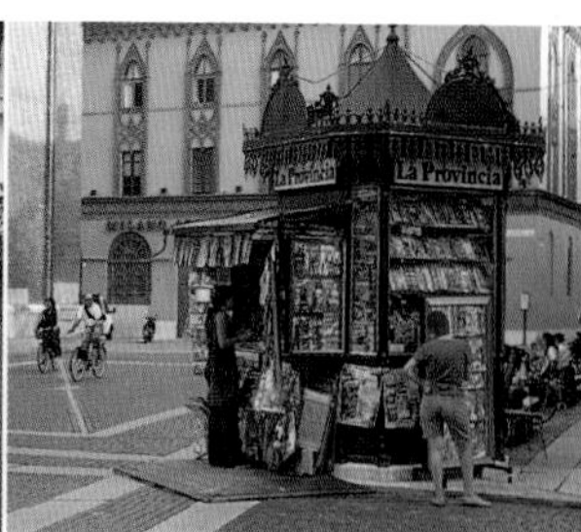

Left **Lake Iseo** Right **Piazza del Comune, Cremona**

Mantua

9 Sabbioneta

Duke Vespasiano Gonzaga had this town built from scratch in the late 16th century, the closest any potentate ever got to fully realizing the ideal Renaissance city. A single ticket lets you in to all the major sights: Palazzo Ducale; Palazzo del Giardino (the summer palace); the fabulous trompe-l'oeil frescoed Galleria; and the Teatro all'Antica, the first purpose-built theatre since antiquity. *Map G6 • Tourist info: Piazza d'Armi 1 • 0375-221-044 • www.iatsabbioneta.org*

10 Cremona

This town is home to some of the world's finest makers of stringed instruments, a craft that reached its pinnacle in the 17th century at the workshop of Antonio Stradivari. It is hardly surprising, then, that Cremona's top sights are fiddle-oriented: the Raccolta dei Violini is a roomful of exquisite 17th- and 18th-century instruments; while Museo Stradivariano displays drawings, models and tools from the great man's workshop. *Map E6 • Tourist info: Piazza del Comune 5 • 0372-406-391 • www.turismocremona.it*

Two Days from Garda to Como

Day One

The smaller lakes and towns are scattered across Lombardy and eastern Piemonte, impossible to see in one short trip, but some of the best can been enjoyed on a leisurely two-day drive from Lake Garda to Lake Como.

Head west on the A4 Autostrada to **Brescia** to spend your first morning admiring its museum and Roman sights. Having lunched at **Trattoria Mezzeria** *(see p129)*, continue to **Lake Iseo**. Explore the eastern shore, especially the Romanino frescoes in Pisogne, the small museum in Lovere and the rock pinnacles outside Cislano.

If you can, spend the night at **I Due Roccoli** *(see p148)*, or at least have dinner there *(p129)*.

Day Two

On Day Two, drive north into the **Val Calmonica** *(see p47)* to view some of the valley's prehistoric rock carvings. Then head back south to diverge west at Lovere for the back road to **Bergamo**.

Check into your hotel and spend the afternoon enjoying the Renaissance architecture and carvings of the Colleoni Chapel, the excellent Accademia Carrara gallery, medieval town square and, of course, the town's shops, cafés and wine bars.

End your day with a hearty meal of local specialities at the **Taverna del Colleoni & dell'Angelo** on the main square *(see p129)*.

Left **I Portici del Comune** Right **Caffè del Tasso**

TOP 10 Shops, Cafés and Nightspots

1 Lagostina, Lake Orta
The discount factory outlet for the famed homewares designer. Get 20–50% off here and at similar outlets on the same road – Bialetti (No. 106) and Fratelli Piazza Effepi (No. 242) – and Alessi (Via Privata Alessi, *see below*). Look for slight irregulars *(sformati)* for bigger savings. *Via IV Novembre 39, Crusinallo-Omegna • Map A3 • 0323-865058*

2 Armani Factory Store, Vertemate
Well worth a visit, for the large discounts (30–50 per cent) on men's and women's clothing. *Via Provinciale per Bergamo 13 • Map D3–4 • 031-887-373*

3 Alessi, Lake Orta
This outlet offers 10% off the current collection of some of the best of Italian industrial design for kitchen and home, but plenty of bargains can be had on seconds and discontinued products. *Via Privata Alessi 6, Crusinallo-Omegna • Map A3 • 032-386-8648*

4 Caffè del Tasso, Bergamo
This historic café has been a local living room (and site of rebellious debates) since the 15th century *(see also p65)*. *Piazza Vecchia 3 • Map D3 • 035-237-966 • €*

5 Colombo Bar, Vigevano
Enjoy an *aperitivo* in one of the most beautiful Renaissance squares in Lombardy. *Piazza Ducale 40 • Map B5 • 038-174-946 • €€€*

6 Corneliani, Mantua
World-renowned for elegant menswear in the finest fabrics, Corneliani offers two floors of bargains, from suits to casuals. It also has footwear, bags, knitwear and accessories. *Via Ostiglia 23 • Map G/H6 • 0376-304410*

7 Cocoricò, Mantua
This popular wine bar is open from 6am until the early hours of the next day. Great for breakfast, a lunchtime snack or a pre-dinner cocktail. *Viale Gorizia 34 • Map H6 • €€*

8 Sperlari, Cremona
Wood-floored shop from 1836 selling its own sweets, *torrone* (nougat), cordials, liqueurs, candied fruits and "cherries with spirit". *Via Solferino 25 • Map E6 • 0372 22346*

9 Caffè Bolla, Como
Between the landing stage and the Duomo, this café is a landmark in a city with myriad bars. Perfect for breakfast, coffee and pre-prandial *aperitivi*. Its ice cream attracts a faithful following *(see also p65)*. *Via Boldoni 6 • Map C3 • 031-264-256 • €€€*

10 I Portici del Comune, Cremona
Good coffee, *gelato* and *panini*. Tables are arranged under an arcade across the piazza from the prettiest Duomo façade in Lombardy *(see also p65)*. *Piazza del Comune 2 • Map E6 • 335-783-6894 • €*

For places to stay around the Smaller Lakes and Towns **see p148**

Price Categories

For a three-course meal for one with half a bottle of wine (or equivalent meal), taxes and extra charges.	
€	under €20
€€	€20–€30
€€€	€30–€40
€€€€	€40–€50
€€€€€	over €50

Left **Taverna del Colleoni & dell'Angelo** Right **I Due Roccoli**

TOP 10 Places to Eat

1 I Due Roccoli, Lake Iseo
The restaurant of an excellent hotel *(see p148)* set high above the town of Iseo. Refined regional food is served on a patio overlooking lawns and woods *(see also p69)*. *Via Silvio Bonomelli, Iseo • Map E4 • 030-982-2977 • Closed Nov–late Mar • €€€€€*

2 Maran, Lake Varese
Trattoria with a lovely terrace offering gorgeous lake views, serving traditional local cuisine based on lake fish and game. *Via E Ponti 63, Calcinate del Pesce, Varese • Map B3 • 0332-310-212 • Closed Tue • No credit cards • €€€*

3 Ai Due Santi, Lake Orta
On the main square, with a fantastic view of Isola San Giulio, this restaurant serves a wide range of regional specialities. *Piazza Motta 18, Orta San Giulio • Map A3 • 0322-90-192 • Closed Wed, Nov • €€€*

4 Villa Crespi, Lake Orta
Stylish restaurant in a unique Moorish-fantasy hotel *(see p148)*. Elegant service and top-quality regional cuisine. *Via G Fava 18, San Giulio • Map A3 • 0322-911-908 • Closed Mon & lunch Tue • €€€€€*

5 Il Volto, Lake Iseo
This trattoria-osteria with one Michelin star has a very pleasant atmosphere, which is as prized as the excellent food. *Via Mirolte 33, Iseo • Map E4 • 030-981-462 • Closed Wed & Thu • €€€*

6 Taverna del Colleoni & dell'Angelo, Bergamo
Formal restaurant installed in an evocative Renaissance *palazzo* on the main piazza, with outdoor dining in summer. Turn to the back of the menu for local specialities. *Piazza Vecchia 7 • Map D3 • 035-232-596 • Closed Mon • €€€€€*

7 Leoncino Rosso, Mantua
A rustic restaurant just off the main square that has been serving Mantuan fare since 1750, such as *tortelli di zucca* (pasta with pumpkin). *Via Giustiziati 33 • Map H6 • 0376-323-277 • Closed dinner Sun, 10 days Feb, 2 wks Aug • €€*

8 Ochina Bianca, Mantua
Distinctive variations on local dishes and a judicious use of fresh fish from the Mincio river. *Via Finzi 2 • Map H6 • 0376-323-700 • €€€€*

9 La Sosta, Cremona
A wood-panelled osteria loved by locals for its home cooking. The *gnocchi vecchia Cremona* (stuffed potato dumplings) is a 17th-century recipe. *Via Sicardo 9 • Map E6 • 0372-456-656 • Closed Mon & dinner Sun, 1 wk Feb, 3 wks Aug • €€€€*

10 Trattoria Mezzeria, Brescia
This busy little family-run restaurant serves *gnocchi di zucca* where potato is replaced with pumpkin as the house speciality. *Via Trieste 66 • Map F4 • 030-40-306 • Closed Sun, Aug • €€€*

***Note:** Unless otherwise stated, all restaurants accept credit cards and serve vegetarian meals*

ALBERGO GARDESANA

STREETSMART

Left **Coach services at Malpensa Airport** Centre **Linate Airport** Right **Arriving by car**

Top 10 Arriving in Milan

1 By Air from the UK

Alitalia, British Airways and easyJet fly into Milan from many UK airports. From Ireland, Aer Lingus flies into Milan Malpensa and Linate. Ryanair flies from Ireland and the UK to Bergamo's Orio al Serio airport which is linked to Milan by bus.

2 By Air from North America

There are direct flights to Milan Malpensa from North American cities on US airlines as well as Italy's Alitalia, but most flights are via Rome. No direct flights from Canada.

3 By Air from Australia

Alitalia flies Sydney to Rome, from where you can transfer to Milan. Qantas flies from various Australian and New Zealand cities to Rome via Bangkok, though it's cheaper to fly via London.

4 By Air from the Continent

The national airlines of many European countries offer flights into one of Milan's three airports. On the continent, Ryanair flies to Milan from Frankfurt-Hahn, Brussels, Paris and Barcelona; Virgin Express flies in from Brussels.

5 Internet Air Bargains

Most airlines use their websites to promote sales and bargain tickets. Expedia and Travelocity collate most regular best fares offered from the US and UK. Booking engines run by airline consortiums include Orbitz in the US and Opodo in Europe. Also check sites such as www.lastminute.com.

6 Malpensa Airport

Closer to Varese than to Milan, the airport is linked by the Malpensa Express to Cadorna station in western Milan (40 mins, leaving every half hour). You can also catch a bus: Malpensa Express or Shuttle (50 mins, 2–3 per hour) to central Milan.

7 Linate Airport

Milan's secondary airport, just east of the city, receives many Alitalia flights as well as those from across Europe. The 73 city bus leaves every half hour for the 25-minute trip to central Milan (buy tickets on the bus). Alternatively, take a taxi into the centre. It's the quickest and easiest option, and not terribly expensive.

8 By Train

From London, you can take the Eurostar to Paris and pick up one of three daily trains to Milan (they take anywhere between 6 hours 30 mins and 10 hours 30 mins). All international services come into Milan's Stazione Centrale.

9 Milan's Train Stations

Most trains arrive at Milan's Stazione Centrale; its tourist office is hidden down a corridor of shops off the arrivals hall. Other stations in Milan include Cadorna, also known as Milano Nord (services to Malpensa airport, Como and Varese), Porta Genova (Asti, Alessandra and other points southwest), and Porta Garibaldi (Lecco).

10 By Car

While many roads to Italy involve crossing the Alps, either by tunnel or via mountain passes, the border crossing at Ventimiglia from the French Riviera and Ponte Tresa or Porto Ceresio from Switzerland are exceptions. *Autostrade* are toll roads, so have cash or cards available.

Directory

Airline Websites
www.alitalia.com
www.ba.com
www.ryanair.com
www.easyjet.com
www.aerlingus.com
www.qantas.com
www.virginexpress.com

Internet Agents
www.expedia.co.uk
www.travelocity.co.uk
www.opodo.co.uk

Milan's Airports
• 02-232-323 • www.sea-aeroportimilano.it
• Orio al Serio, Bergamo; www.sacbo.it

Previous pages **Torri del Benaco, Lake Garda**

Left **Coach tour** Centre **Road sign** Right **Ferry**

TOP 10 Getting Around Milan & the Lakes

1 By Train

Italian trains, run by Trenitalia, are speedy and efficient, but don't cover every Lombard corner. Each station posts its own schedule – departures on yellow, arrivals on white – and newsstands sell national schedules. Ticket lines can be long (automated machines now help), and strikes (*sciopero*) annoyingly frequent. You must validate your ticket at the station's or track's yellow box before boarding.

2 By Coach (Long-Distance Bus)

Coaches (pullman) are a good way of travelling around the lakes. They are best used to reach destinations where trains don't go and the service is frequent.

3 By Ferry

Lakes Como, Garda, Maggiore and Iseo each have a public ferry system run by Navigazione Laghi. The smaller lakes have skiffs connecting towns or running out to islands. Private boats and water taxis charge at least twice as much as public boats.

4 By Rental Car

The best way to explore the environs. Local outfits are rarely cheaper than international agents, and arranging a rental from your home country is invariably the best option. Most companies require a theft protection charge. Your credit card may cover this automatically. Rental companies' offices can be found inside the Stazione Centrale.

5 Road Signs and Maps

TCI (Touring Club Italiano) maps are widely available in Italy. Michelin maps offer more sightseeing indications, including scenic roads highlighted in green. Italian road signs (green for Autostrada highways, blue for state roads) show destinations more often than route numbers. Signage can be erratic. Take extra care at motorway exits.

6 Road Rules

Speed limits: 30–50 kmh (20–30 mph) in town; 80–110 kmh (50–70 mph) on two-lane roads; and 130 kmh (80 mph) on highways. Speed control cameras automatically generate tickets for speeding violations.

7 Tolls and Fuel

Lombardy's only toll roads are the autostrade connecting the main cities. Unleaded petrol is *senza piombo* or *verde*; diesel is *gasolio*. Though most stations close Saturday afternoon and Sundays, many have pumps that accept notes and cards.

8 Parking

Though few hotels have their own parking, many have agreements with local garages. Round blue signs with a red slash mean no parking. Legal parking is always marked: white-lined spaces are free; yellow-lined spaces are restricted to residents only and blue spaces available for an hourly fee.

9 City Bus, Tram and Metro

Milan has a mix of transport: buses, trams and an underground, and all use the same tickets. Buy them at tobacconists (*tabacchi*, indicated by a white-on-brown "T" sign), newsstands (*edicola*), or bars. Stamp one end on the tram or bus. They are valid for 90 minutes during which time you may transfer. A 24-hour ticket costs €4.50.

10 Taxis

You'll find taxi ranks at airports and stations. Any hotel or restaurant will know the local Radio Taxi number to call for you. Standard rates go up with luggage, after 8pm, on Sundays, and for trips outside the centre.

Directory

Trains
www.trenitalia.com
www.trenord.it

Ferries
www.navlaghi.it

Car Rentals
www.europebycar.com
www.autoeurope.com
www.holidayautos.co.uk

For leasing a car over a period of more than three weeks **see p135**

Left **Tourist Board** Centre **Shopping arcade** Right **Newsagent**

TOP 10 General Information

1 Italian State Tourism Board
Provincial tourism boards control most information and ENIT (Ente Nazionale Italiano per il Turismo), the national tourist office, has links to the local Lombardy tourist boards on their website.

2 Tourist Offices in Lombardy
Local *informazioni turistiche* offices, often indicated as "IAT" or "Pro Loco", are good for free maps, sight and museum opening hours, hotel directories and cultural events. Milan's tourist office is at Piazza del Castello 1 (02-7740-4343), with a branch in Stazione Centrale (02-7740-4318).

3 Immigration Laws
Citizens of the UK, Ireland, US, Canada, New Zealand and Australia need only a valid passport to visit Italy for up to 90 days for tourism.

4 Customs
You may bring into Italy personal items with the following quirky limits: 400 cigarettes (or 550 grammes of tobacco), 2 cameras, 10 rolls of film, a pair of skis, two tennis rackets, one shooting gun with 200 cartridges and a litre of alcohol.

5 Opening Hours
Food shops open at 8:30am while other shops and businesses open at 9:30am, shut for *riposo* from about 1pm to 3 or 3:30pm (state museums and churches, too), and close around 7:30pm. Hairdressers are closed on Mondays. In larger cities, the *riposo* is disappearing in favour of *orario continuato*, working straight through.

6 Electricity and Outlets
Italy is on 220V/50 cycles. To operate a 110V device you need a converter (most laptops and camcorders have this built in). To plug it in, you need an adapter from your pronged plugs to Continental Europe's two round pins.

7 TV & Newspapers
Most hotels 3-stars and above get satellite TV with CNN and BBC news. Train station and central piazza newsstands are best for finding English-language newspapers (the *International Herald Tribune* comes with an *Italy Daily* insert). *Informer* (www.informer.it) is Milan's ex-pat English-language magazine.

8 When to Go
Lombardy has a mild climate, hotter and with less rainfall than most of the UK. August heat can be oppressive, while January snow is common. Spring's middle ground keeps hotels booked in the cities, but summer is the season for the lakes. There is winter skiing in the Alps with an all-year ski resort at Bormio.

9 High Season and Holidays
High season is Easter–Jul and Sep–Oct. But while cities are deserted mid- to late Aug, lakeside resorts are packed through Jul–Aug. Milan's trade fairs (Mar, Apr, Oct) make finding hotel rooms and dinner reservations difficult. National holidays are: 1 & 6 Jan, Easter Sun & Mon, 25 Apr, 1 May, 2 Jun, 15 Aug, 1 Nov, and 7 (Milan only), 8, 25 & 26 Dec.

10 What to Pack
Italians dress well, so it's a good idea to take at least one nice outfit, though few restaurants require jacket and tie. Many churches do not allow bare knees or shoulders (no shorts, miniskirts, or vests).

Tourism Websites

- *Italian Tourist Board: www.enit.it*
- *Lombardy: www.turismo.regione.lombardia.it*
- *Piemonte: www.regione.piemonte.it/turismo*
- *Milan: www.visitamilano.it*
- *Garda: www.lakegarda.com*
- *Como: www.lakecomo.org*
- *Maggiore: www.illagomaggiore.com*

Left **Sightseers** Centre **One-star hotel** Right **Local craft stall**

Top 10 Ways to Save Money

1 Sightseeing for Free

Lombardy's churches are free, and contain some of Italy's greatest art and architecture. The best chapels often charge admission, however. Italy's gorgeous, *palazzo*-rimmed squares are free "theatres of life".

2 Sightseeing at a Discount

Discount admission to sights and museums varies greatly: the age cut-off may be 6, 12, 14, or 18, or just "students" and seniors (over 60 or sometimes 65). National museums are free to those under 18 and over 60 (EU citizens). Many towns now sell tickets that combine several sights.

3 Travel Discounts

Under 26s can buy a Carta Verde for about €40 and receive 10 per cent discount on any Italian train ticket; the same deal for over 60s is called Carta Argento. But none of Italy's rail passes will pay off financially if you're sticking just to Lombardy.

4 Lease a Car

For periods longer than 21 days, a short-term lease is often cheaper than renting a car. Unlike with rentals, you also get full insurance coverage with no deductable, plus a brand-new car straight from the factory. The pioneers in this arrangement are Europe By Car and Auto Europe *(see p133)*, though other agencies are starting to pick up on the concept.

5 Save Money on Accommodation

While in tourist towns a lesser star rating will mean lower prices with an acceptable drop in standards, in places where most travel is for business, such as Milan, this does not apply. In addition to the Budget Gems listed on p147, you can try for weekend discounts.

6 Cheap Eats

In food-loving Italy, price or category of restaurant has little to do with the quality of food, so a cheaper *osteria* or trattoria can be as tasty an option as a fancy ristorante. Be aware that appetizers tend to cost almost as much as first courses, but tap water *(acqua dal rubinetto)* is usually free. *Tavole calde* and bars *(see p142)* offer super cheap hot meals.

7 Have a Picnic

For little money, you can visit a string of small delis *(alimentari)*, greengrocers *(fruttivendolo)*, bread and pastry shops *(panetteria/pasticceria)*, and wine stores *(enoteca/fiaschetteria)* and create your own picnic fit for a king. Then choose your location – overlooking a lake, or in a town's main square, perhaps.

8 Pay in Cash

Cash will often get you a discount in shops and smaller hotels, as they won't have to pay a credit card commission. However, make sure you leave with some kind of receipt, as by law you have to carry it 400 m beyond the store (a whole branch of the Italian police is devoted to financial fraud).

9 Visit in the Off-Season

Spring and now autumn too are getting more crowded than summer, and hotels and airlines often extend their high-season prices accordingly. Mid-Nov to just before Easter is low season in Italy, when rates on air fares and hotels can drop considerably. However, facilities around the lakes (especially in resort towns) almost completely shut down in winter.

10 Shop Wisely

When possible, non-EU visitors should save purchasing for one store to hurdle the VAT limit and get a refund *(see p137)*. Go for artisan products rather than souvenirs, and, if you can, purchase directly from the craftspeople. Also, buy what you can't get in your home country – look for local produce. Also, be sure to watch out for counterfeit banknotes, especially for ones above the €50 denomination.

Left **ATM sign** Centre **Telephone kiosks** Right **Internet café**

Top 10 Banking and Communications

1 Exchanging Money

If you can't use an ATM *(bancomat)* to get cash, change money at a bank (or, for American Express card-holders, an Amex office) for the next-best rates and lowest charges. Take your passport as ID. "Cambio" exchange booths are open longer, but have worse rates. Shops and hotels generally offer poor rates for traveller's cheques.

2 ATMs

The fastest, easiest and cheapest way to get local currency is via an ATM, drawing money directly from your home current account (savings accounts are not so easily accessed).

3 Credit Cards

MasterCard and Visa are the most widely accepted – just about everywhere except the smallest family-run shops, trattorie and hotels. American Express and Diner's Club are less well accepted. You can get credit card cash advances from ATMs, but, unlike with purchases, interest is accrued immediately.

4 Traveller's Cheques

While still the safest way to carry money, traveller's cheques are doomed by the evolution of easier and cheaper ATMs. However, a few cheques are good for emergencies. Buy them denominated in euros. Note that personal cheques are useless, except for Amex card-holders, who can cash cheques at American Express offices.

5 Currency

Italy has joined most of Continental Europe in adopting the Euro (€), which replaced the lira. Euro coins come in €1 and €2, and in 1, 2, 5, 10, 20, and 50 euro cents. Bills come in €5, €10, €20, €50, €100, €200, and €500.

6 Public Phones

Most pay phones in Italy now accept only pre-paid phone cards *(scheda telefonica)* you can buy in several denominations at tobacconists *(tabacchi)* and newsstands. Break off the corner before inserting it. There is also a range of pre-paid *carta telefonica internazionale* that give you a number to call and a code for international calls.

7 Calling Home

Arranging to take a call in your hotel room is invariably cheaper than using the Italian phone system. But if you want to make an outward call, use the cards described above or international phone booths in major post offices. To reverse charges, dial the international operator at 170. Calls can usually be placed at hotels, but the charges are excessive. To call Italy from abroad, dial your international prefix (011 in the US, 00 in most other countries), then Italy's country code of 39, followed by the number, including that initial zero (which, formerly, was dropped).

8 Internet Access

Internet cafés are forever popping up and disappearing with equal alacrity (ask at the tourist office if you don't stumble upon any). Free Wi-Fi is available in and outside of most public buildings.

9 Postal Service

To send postcards and letters, just ask any tobacconist *(tabacchi)* or newsagent for stamps *(francobolli)* for the country to which you are mailing. Then drop the post in the slot of the mail box (usually red) labelled "*per tutte le altre destinazioni*" (not "*per la città*").

10 Receiving Mail

Mail addressed to "[Your Name] / Fermo Posta / [Town Name], Italia / ITALY" should make it to the main local post office (though it helps to add the postal code, if you can find it). There's a small fee to pick it up, though Amex card-holders can receive free of charge letters sent to "[Your Name] / Client Mail / American Express / Via Brera 3 / 20121 Milano, Italia / ITALY".

Left **Shopping street** Centre **Bottles of Chianti** Right **Local ceramic craft**

Top 10 Shopping Tips

1 Shop Hours

Shops open around 9:30am and close around 7:30pm, with long afternoon breaks *(see p134)*.

2 Haggling

Bartering over price is the life-blood of markets, but isn't the norm in the majority of shops. Many market stallholders now hail from Middle Eastern countries where bargaining is an art form, so be ready to go through the full ritual: you acting less and less interested, the stallholder acting more and more offended.

3 Tax Refunds

Italy's Value Added Tax (IVA) is included in the price tag of every item. Non-EU visitors who spend more than €155 in one shop can get the tax refunded. Ask the store to help you fill in the forms; then bring them and the receipts to the customs office at the airport to complete the paperwork. Your refund will be mailed (though it may take some months). Stores marked "Tax Free Shopping for Tourists" speed up the process, giving you a cheque for the customs office to stamp, which can then be redeemed at the airport's Tax Free Shopping desk.

4 Customs Limits

UK and Irish citizens can bring home virtually anything duty free (though, in principle, limits such as no more than 90 litres of wine apply). US citizens are limited to $400 worth of goods duty-free, including 1 litre of alcohol, 200 cigarettes and 100 cigars. Canadian, Australian, and New Zealand limitations are roughly similar. Unless you are from the EU, you are not allowed to take home flowers, bulbs, fruits, vegetables, meats (unless tinned) and cheeses runnier than brie.

5 Fashion

One of the world's elite capitals of fashion, Milan is home to many top names in haute couture: Prada, Armani, Versace, Krizia, Missoni and Ferré, to name but a few. In March and October, supermodels draped in next season's fashions parade the runways in the fashion shows. Top couture isn't likely to be any cheaper in Milan (unless you go to a discount outlet), but buying clothes here has a certain cachet.

6 Design Objects

Italians are masters of industrial design, from Ferraris to funky Alessi tea kettles. So if the Ferrari doesn't fit your budget, consider some elegant or quirky kitchenware instead.

7 Bargain Hunting

For craftware, such as ceramics, carved wood and even leather shoes, try to visit the workshops and buy at source. For everything else, use the Italian shopper's three cardinal "S"s: *sconti* (reduced prices), *saldi* (sales), and *spacci* (discount outlets).

8 Ship Your Souvenirs

Rather than carry your perhaps bulky purchases all around Lombardy, see if the shop can ship them home for you on the spot. The fee is often worth the hassle saved. If you have a rental car big enough to store your goods, you could try the other tack: at the end of your trip post home your dirty laundry and anything you won't miss for a while, then use the space saved to pack your souvenirs.

9 Wine

Italy's best souvenir, though rather heavy (and US citizens can only take home one bottle without paying a duty). Shipping is expensive, so save it for when you discover a small vineyard whose wines aren't exported and buy a whole case.

10 Crafts

Italy is renowned for the quality of its hand-painted ceramics – souvenirs that have a practical use as well as an aesthetic appeal. Milan is also home to fine jewellers, from big names such as Bulgari to artisans labouring in small boutiques.

Left **Ambulance** Centre **Farmacia sign** Right **Trams**

Top 10 Health and Safety Tips

1 Emergencies

You can dial 113 for general emergencies: see the Directory for more specific numbers. Note that the car breakdown number is a pay towing service.

2 Safety

Italians do tend to drive aggressively, so be attentive behind the wheel. Also, take steps to avoid pickpockets *(see below)*. Women (especially young foreign women) may be pestered, but it's mostly harmless. Apart from these things, Italy is a remarkably safe country, and violent crime is rare.

3 Pickpockets

On crowded trams and buses, the metro, and around train stations and other areas where tourists congregate, pickpockets will be at work. Keep your wits about you and ensure your passport, credit cards, plane tickets and money are well hidden.

4 Street Beggars

Every European city has its street beggars and master pickpockets, and Milan is no exception. Begging varies from the apathetic seated figure with a tin for change to the confrontational and occasionally aggressive street-hardened homeless person. A common pickpocketing technique is to use distraction, such as crowding you or using a cardboard sign to disguise the act of thievery. But, despite this, begging and street crime are not especially rife in Milan.

5 Scams

While not particularly rampant, scams are sometimes attempted on the most clueless-seeming of tourists. Taxis might try to set the meter for "out of town" rates rather than local. Restaurants might try to pad the bill with items not ordered, and are the mostly likely to try and double-charge your credit card. Just be attentive, and the unscrupulous are unlikely to try.

6 The Police

There are two main police branches: the regular Polizia and the military-trained national Carabinieri force. A police office is called a *questura*.

7 Medical Charges

It's sensible to take out medical insurance, even if your country has a reciprocal agreement with Italy. Usually you must pay any hospital charges up front and apply for reimbursement when you get home. US Blue Cross/Blue Shield members can visit affiliated hospitals in Italy, using their card as at home.

8 Italian Hospitals

Italian hospitals *(ospedale)* are efficient and semi-privatized. The emergency room is called *pronto soccorso*. Unless you're admitted overnight, they'll usually give you a check-up, write a prescription and send you off with a smile, no paperwork involved.

9 Pharmacies

Italian *farmacie* are usually well equipped and excellent in helping with minor ailments. They take turns to stay open at night and on Sunday – the information will be posted on the window. Otherwise, head for the 24-hour pharmacy in Milan's Stazione Centrale train station.

10 Food and Water Safety

Italian water is safe to drink everywhere except on trains and any source signposted *"aqua non potabile"*. Food is largely safe, though uncooked seafood is always risky.

Directory

Emergency Numbers
- *General 113*
- *Ambulance 118*
- *Fire 115*
- *Car breakdown 116*

Police
- *Regular Polizia 113*
- *Carabinieri 112*

Blue Cross
www.bluecross.com

24-hour Pharmacy
Stazione Centrale, Milan • 02-669-0735

Left **Hôtel des Iles Borromées, Lake Maggiore** Centre **Cheap fashion** Right **Central Milan traffic**

Top 10 Things to Avoid

1 Milan in August

August in Milan can be brutally hot, and almost the whole city goes on holiday, including many pharmacists and grocers. However, most tourist attractions and shops in the centre, as well as Navigli's restaurants and night spots, remain open, many with air conditioning. Bring mosquito repellent.

2 The Lakes in Winter

Most hotels shut down from October or November through to February, many reopening only at Easter. Only Lake Maggiore keeps a longer season, with many of its inns and restaurants closing only for December or January.

3 Not Booking a Milan Hotel During Trade Fairs

The usual tourist seasons don't apply to business-orientated Milan. The months to watch out for are March, April and October when major trade fairs and fashion shows keep even the most basic, one-star hotels booked solid. Even outside these months, it can be difficult to find a room. It's always wise to book ahead.

4 Full Pension Hotel Rates

Hotels on the lakes often cater largely to habitual holidaymakers who stay a week or more and rarely budge from their chosen tanning spots. The package deals they try to force on clients reflect this; some require stays of three nights, many insist you take at least a half-board deal. Try to negotiate more leeway.

5 Driving in Milan

A car is utterly unnecessary in Milan: some roads are now pedestrianized; when it is available, parking is limited and expensive (cars entering the centre are also subject to a congestion charge, the Area C); and to the uninitiated, traffic seems to move very fast. Car hire makes sense only for touring around the lakes.

6 Not Reserving Tickets for the Last Supper

If you do not book ahead to visit Leonardo's *Last Supper* *(see pp8–9)*, you will be turned away at the door. Try to reserve as far in advance as possible (ideally at least 6 weeks). This is not an exaggeration.

7 Overloading Your Itinerary

It might make sense to visit Milan's museums and monuments back-to-back, but once you get up to the lakes, it is time to take it easy. Enjoy the Italian art of *dolce far niente*, the "sweetness of doing nothing".

8 Boutique Price Tags

Window shopping amid the renowned boutiques of Milan's Quadrilatero d'Oro can be fun, but few visitors really have deep enough pockets to turn browsing into a new wardrobe. Luckily, this epicentre of high fashion has also spawned a thriving business of *spacci* (stock houses) where you can get last year's fashions, slight irregulars and odd sizes at 30% to 50% off the usual price tags *(see also p137)*.

9 Wearing a Waist Pack

Despite being sold on its seeming convenience for the luggage-laden traveller, the waist pack is arguably the worst travel accessory ever invented. It places all of your most important belongings at the perfect height for a light-fingered thief to rifle through at his or her leisure.

10 Gardaland Without Children

Though Gardaland may be Italy's best theme park and deserving of a recommendation as a top attraction for kids *(see pp63 & 117)*, bear in mind that Italy isn't renowned for its theme parks. So while it is vaunted as one of Lake Garda's largest individual "sights", it isn't worthwhile unless you have bored children or you love all things kitsch.

Left **Student travellers** Right **Senior visitors**

Top 10 Travellers with Special Concerns

1 Tips for Students

Milan has a vast student population spanning a wider age range than their British or US counterparts. Many hang out in bars at Navigli, and in clubs in Ticinese. They're also habitués of the bars in the Brera neighbourhood. To get discounts when sightseeing, ask for "sconto per studenti".

2 Resources for Students

Remember to take your ISIC (International Student Identity Card), the only card widely accepted as proof of status.

3 Tips for the Elderly

Discounts for *anziani* (pensioners) are often available at sights and on transport *(see p135)*.

4 Resources for the Elderly

Besides books and magazines devoted to the mature traveller, you can get good travel information, advice on tour operators, and sometimes discounts, from the major national associations for retired persons, such as ARP (UK) and AARP (US).

5 Tips for Women

The "Latin Lover" is alive and well, and women may receive more attention than they are used to. Behaviour like open staring, verbal come-ons, even bottom-pinching is not uncommon. Be firm, to stop it in its tracks.

6 Resources for Women

There are few official resources for women, other than some clubs for ex-pats and visitors: the Benvenuto Club for social activities, and the PWA (Professional Women's Association), for career networking.Try www.journeywoman.com for travelling tips.

7 Tips for the Disabled

Preservation laws deter owners from altering the city's older buildings in order to accommodate wheelchairs. However, most major museums have disabled access, and many hotels have a few wheelchair-friendly rooms. Most Metro stops are wheelchair accessible, but restaurant toilets may not be. Milanopertutti gives detailed accessibility information in English.

8 Resources for the Disabled

RADAR (the Royal Association for Disability and Rehabilitation) in London publishes a series of useful pamphlets. Join Holiday Care Service, in Surrey, for advice on disabled-friendly accommodation.

9 Tips for Gay and Lesbian Travellers

Homosexuality is broadly accepted in as cosmopolitan a city as Milan, which hosted the World Pride festival in 2000. Moderate physical affection will draw little undue attention.

10 Resources for Gays & Lesbians

Italy's national organization for homosexuals (curiously, a subset of the National Communist Youth Alliance) is ARCI-Gay; the lesbian branch is ARCI-Lesbica. Milan's gay bookshop is Libreria Babele; there are gay travel guides put out by Ferrari, Spartacus and Frommer's. A useful website is www.gay.it.

Directory

Students
- *STA Travel, 0871-230-0044, www.statravel.co.uk*
- *Travel CUTS, www.travelcuts.com*

Seniors
- *ARP, 020-8764-3344*
- *AARP, 800-424-3410, www.aarp.org*

Women
- *www.pwa-milan.org*

Disabled
- *RADAR, 020-7250-3222, www.radar.org.uk*
- *Holiday Care Service, 01293-774-535*
- *www.milanopertutti.it*

Gay/Lesbian
- *ARCI-Gay, 02-5412-2225, www.arcigaymilano.org*
- *ARCI-Lesbica, 02-2901-4027, www.arcilesbica.it*

Left **Sightseeing tour** Right **Station concourse**

Top 10 Tips for Families

1 Try Picnicking
It saves money, makes for a fun outing, gives children a chance to pick out what they want from the wonderful delis and bakers, and also gives them a break from all those restaurants where they have to be on best behaviour – though this is, in fact, less of an issue in Italy. Also, since travelling with children slows you down in many ways, picnic lunches (always quicker than sitting down to a three-course meal) help make up some lost time.

2 Order Half-Portions
A *mezza porzione* for smaller appetites costs 30–50 per cent less than a full portion. Those feeling weighed down by all this great Italian food, who yet feel compelled to continue trying it all can cash in on this tip. Sharing a plate (*uno in due*) is also an option.

3 Share a Room
Rather than booking two separate rooms for parents and kids, trade some privacy for savings and bunk the whole clan in one room. Each extra bed costs no more than 35 per cent extra on the price of a double; cots and baby cribs are even less. But if some time apart is the only route to familial peace, ask for family suites or rooms sharing a common door.

4 Make a Home-Base
Try to stay in one hotel or apartment if possible, and make day-trips rather than moving on from one town to the next. The constant upheaval can be exhausting for kids, changing hotels is time-consuming and rates for stays of three days or longer are usually reduced.

5 Sightseeing Discounts
Ridotto is the word for reduced-price tickets, which may apply to all students or at least the under 18s. A few sights offer a *biglietto famiglia* for family group discount. Admission may be free under the age of 6, 12 or even 18 (especially for EU citizens).

6 Train Discounts
Those under 27 can buy a Carta Verde from train stations to save 20 per cent on tickets.

7 Rent a Car
Renting one mid-sized car is far cheaper than four or even three sets of train tickets, and has the added benefit of allowing you more flexibility in terms of itinerary and speed *(see p133)*.

8 Gelato Breaks
Don't over-pack your itinerary. Skip a few museums, reduce the number of gardens you plan to visit and take time to enjoy some delicious Italian ice cream instead.

9 Use Riposo Wisely
Sightseeing is exhausting. Therefore, do as the Italians do, and take a *riposo* (a nap) after lunch rather than trying to pack still more sights into your holiday schedule.

10 Enjoy Italy's family culture
Italy's is a multigenerational culture, accustomed to welcoming large family groups all travelling together. And a visiting child attempting to speak a little Italian can be a great icebreaker.

Gelateria

Left **Formal dinner placings** Centre **A friendly waiter** Right **Dishes at a tavola calda**

Top 10 Tips for Eating Out

1 Restaurant Types

A ristorante is the most formal, expensive, eatery; a trattoria a family-run, moderately priced joint; an *osteria* anything from a simple trattoria to the equivalent of a pub with dishes of cured meats and cheeses. However, such distinctions are slowly dissolving.

2 The Italian Meal

Italian meals, especially dinners, are drawn-out affairs of two to four hours, with the courses listed below followed by an espresso and digestive liqueur *(digestivo)* such as grappa. Lunch used to be similar but life's modern pace is shortening it. Breakfast is traditionally an espresso or cappuccino with a sweetened roll or croissant (*brioche* or *cornetto*).

3 Antipasto

This is the appetizer course. A typical offering would be bruschetta (toasted bread rubbed with garlic, olive oil, salt, and sometimes tomatoes) and/or cured meats such as prosciutto, salami, bresaola (thin slices of dried beef) and carpaccio (wafer-thin raw beef). Also popular are *nervetti* (a cold salad of pickled calf tendons) or a caprese salad of tomatoes and mozzarella.

4 Primo

The first course. Risotto (creamy arborio rice) is usually studded with seasonal vegetables, sausage bits *(alla mantovana)*, or sometimes a seafood medley. Pastas include *tortelli di zucca* (pumpkin-stuffed pockets), *strangolapreti* (balls of ricotta and spinach), *agnolotti* (tiny, meat-filled ravioli), and *pizzoccheri* (a casserole of buckwheat pasta layered with cheese, potatoes and cabbage). Soups *(minestre)* include minestrone (vegetable soup), simple *zuppa pavese* (bread and eggs in broth), and *cassoeûla* *(see p66)*.

5 Secondo

The main course. Meats include *bistecca* or *manzo* (beef), *vitello* (veal), *agnello/abbacchio* (mutton/spring lamb), *pollo* (chicken), *maiale* (pork), *cinghiale* (boar), *coniglio* (rabbit), and *anatra* (duck). A *Cotoletta* is cutlet, usually veal; a *braciola* is a chop, usually pork. A *grigliata mista* is a hearty mixed meat platter. Local dishes use lake fish *(see p67)*. Order vegetables separately.

6 Dolce

The dessert. Most popular are hard almond biscuits with sweet wine for dunking, lemon sorbet *(sorbetto)*, or *gelato* (ice cream). Egg custards are also favourites, as is *tiramisù* (a rich dessert with espresso and mascarpone cheese). A *macedonia* is a diced fresh fruit cup.

7 Wine and Water

No Italian meal is complete without red *(rosso)* or white *(bianco)* wine *(vino)*; either a carafe *(un litro)* or a half-carafe *(mezzo litro)* of the usually excellent house wine *(vino della casa)*, or a bottle of the good stuff. Italians temper their wine by drinking equal amounts of water, either fizzy *(gassata, frizzante)* or still *(naturale)*.

8 Cover Charges and Tipping

The *pane e coperto* (bread and cover) charge of €1 to €4 per person is unavoidable. If the menu says *"servizio incluso"*, service charge is built in – though it is customary to round up the bill. If not, tip a discretionary 10 to 15 per cent.

9 Restaurant Etiquette

Jacket and tie are rarely required. Waiters expect you to linger over your meal, and won't bring the bill until asked ("il conto per favore").

10 Bars and Tavole Calde

Most Italian bars serve sandwiches and pastries, a morning cappuccino and *cornetto* (also known as *brioche*), espresso throughout the day and apéritifs in the evening. A *tavola calda* is a glorified bar with pre-prepared dishes steaming in trays behind a glass counter.

Left **Hotel room** Centre **Camping site** Right **Hostel in Menaggio**

TOP 10 Accommodation Tips

1 Hotels

Italian hotels are categorised from one-star (basic) to five-stars (deluxe), based largely on the amenities offered rather than charm, historic setting, or location. The star system does not necessarily correspond to that of other countries. At three stars or above, rooms have a private bathroom, TV and phone.

2 Agriturismi (Farm Stays)

Some farms – usually vineyards – offer rooms. This provides inexpensive lodgings in bucolic settings. Some are luxury, some very rustic. Agriturist, Terra Nostra and Turismo Verde are the main consortiums.

3 Villa Companies

Top villa rental agencies in the UK include International Chapters and Cottages to Castles. In the US, try Marjorie Shaw's Insider's Italy, the Parker Company and Villas International.

4 Choosing a Villa

Ask for a schematic layout and as many pictures as possible of the interior and exterior of the apartment/villa and the grounds. Find out how many others might share the villa or other houses on the complex.

5 Rooms to Rent

The tourist office has a list of these invariably cheap options. They can range from a lovely room with semi-private access to a cramped spare bedroom in someone's modern apartment. It can be a great way to meet locals.

6 Camping and Caravaning

Camp sites *(campeggi)* are widespread, but you end up paying almost as much as for a cheap hotel: a fee per person, for your vehicle and for the pitch itself *(see p149)*.

7 Hostels

All cities and major towns have cheap beds in shared dorms. Full of international students, they usually impose a curfew of midnight or so. Most official IYHA (AIG in Italy) hostels are on the edges of towns.

8 Should You Reserve?

Making a reservation in advance is always wise, especially for the first night of your stay and particularly if you have your heart set on a special hotel. The best-known can book up months in advance. However, if you are not fussy, you should be able to find a room when you arrive, at most times of year you visit.

9 Booking Services

For a small fee, most tourist offices and private hotel consortiums will help you find a room. Their offices are usually located in the main train stations and airports. So far, the countless Internet booking services have highly erratic stables of hotels in their databases.

10 Quirks that can Affect the Price

Rooms without private bath, without a view, or for stays longer than three days, often come cheaper. An extra bed in a room usually costs 30–35 per cent more. Breakfast may not be included or may cost €30 extra; parking may be extra; and prices on minibar items and phone calls are often quite exorbitant.

Directory

Agriturismi

- *www.agriturist.it*
- *www.terranostra.it*
- *www.turismoverde.it*

Villas

- *International Chapters, (020) 7722-0722, www.internationalchapters.com*
- *Cottages to Castles, (01622) 775217, www.cottagestocastles.com*
- *Marjorie Shaw's Insider's Italy, www.insidersitaly.com*
- *The Parker Company, (800) 280-2811, www.theparkercompany.com*
- *Villas International, (800) 221-2260, www.villasintl.com*

Hostels

- *www.hostels.com*
- *www.ostelli.it*

Left **Grand Hotel et de Milan** Right **Principe di Savoia**

TOP 10 Milan's Luxury Hotels

1 Four Seasons

This hotel was converted in 1993 from a 15th-century convent, complete with some frescoes. The superior rooms are on the street side, while deluxe rooms open onto the cloisters. Milan's best shops are nearby, and there are two restaurants, one offering a vegetarian menu. *Via Gesù 8 • Map N2 • 02-77-088 • www.fourseasons.com/milan • €€€€€*

2 Grand Hotel et de Milan

The Grand has been Milan's most intimate luxury hotel since 1863, a darling of inveterate shoppers and La Scala stars (it was Callas's Milan home). Composer Giuseppe Verdi was resident for 30 years. *Via Manzoni 29 • Map M3 • 02-723-141 • www.grandhoteletdemilan.it • €€€€€*

3 Park Hyatt Milan

This luxurious hotel is situated in the heart of the city, just steps from Piazza Duomo and the Scala opera house, and within easy access to Via Montenapoleone's shops. The Ed Tuttle-designed interior features Bang & Olufsen TVs, large marble bathrooms and walk-in closets. There is also a spa with a small fitness centre and two steam rooms. *Via Tommaso Grossi 1 • Map L3 • 02-8821-1234 • www.milan.park.hyatt.com • €€€€€*

4 Hotel de la Ville

This hotel is between the Duomo and stylish Via Montenapoleone. The bar, Il Visconteo, is popular for pre-dinner drinks. The rooms feature 18th-century-style antiques. *Via Hoepli 6 • Map M3 • 02-879-1311 • www.hoteldelavillemilano.com • €€€€€*

5 Principe di Savoia

Built in 1927 in a Neo-Classical Lombard style, this is the most elegant of Milan's top hotels. Its Principe Tower was built in 2000 for businessmen who like their modern office conveniences in an old-fashioned atmosphere. *Piazza della Repubblica 17 • Map N1 • 02-623-0555 • www.hotelprincipedisavoia.com • €€€€€*

6 Spadari al Duomo

This gem, filled with original works by contemporary artists, is near Piazza Duomo. Stylish rooms include features such as marble sinks and hydromassage shower stalls. *Via Spadari 11 • Map L4 • 02-7200-2371 • www.spadarihotel.com • €€€€€*

7 Antica Locanda dei Mercanti

This converted apartment between the Duomo and Castello is a wonderful home-away-from-home. The quiet rooms have floral draperies, matching headboards and the occasional exposed beam. The more expensive *terrazzo* rooms have small terraces and canopy beds. There is also a small restaurant and bar. *Via San Tomaso 6 • Map L3 • 02-805-4080 • www.locanda.it • €€€€*

8 Sheraton Diana Majestic

A Liberty-style hotel focused on a lush courtyard garden. The rooms have a modern elegance with such top-end amenities as Bose stereos. *Viale Piave 42 • Map P2 • 02-20-581 • www.sheratondianamajestic.com • €€€€€*

9 Manzoni

Set in a quiet location, the elegant four-star Manzoni offers good value for a hotel in the heart of the city, near the Duomo, La Scala and the main shopping streets. Comfortable rooms have luxurious furnishings. There is also a Wellness Centre and a restaurant serving Milanese dishes. Closed three weeks in August. *Via Santo Spirito • Map N2 • 02-7600-5700 • www.hotelmanzoni.com • €€€€€*

10 Carlton Hotel Baglioni

This hotel on the north side of the shopping district has 19th-century-style silk brocades and inlaid furnishings. There is also a business centre, a spa and a restaurant. *Via Senato 5 • Map N2 • 02-77-077 • www.baglionihotels.com • €€€€€*

***Note:** Unless otherwise stated, all hotels accept credit cards, have en-suite bathrooms and A/C (air conditioning)*

Le Meridien Hotel Gallia

Price Categories

For a standard, double room per night (with breakfast if included), taxes and extra charges.		
	€	under €110
	€€	€110–€160
	€€€	€160–€210
	€€€€	€210–€270
	€€€€€	over €270

Top 10 Milan's Best Business Hotels

1 Le Meridien Hotel Gallia

This bastion of sophistication knits together the best of both worlds: genuine 1937 Liberty-style class with modern comforts and amenities. The rooms have a quirky elegance, the baths are marble-clad, and the dual phone lines have a PC hook-up. Ten conference rooms are so well-equipped there are even simultaneous translators. The solo business traveller will thrill at the extra-wide single beds – uncommon in Italy. *Piazzale Duca d'Aosta 9 • 02-678-51 • www.lemeridiengallia.com • €€€€*

2 Westin Palace

The general decor is a genteel Empire style, but the"smart rooms" have high-tech facilities, and the plush business centre has on-staff translators and 13 well-equipped conference rooms. There is also a fully equipped gym. *Piazza della Repubblica 20 • Map N1 • 02-63-361 • www.westinpalacemilan.com • €€€€€*

3 Una Hotel Century

Near the central station, north of Piazza della Repubblica, this property is made up entirely of business suites: 144 sleek, modern units, each with a bedroom and separate living room/office. *Via F Filzi 25B • 02-675-041 • www.unahotels.it • €€€*

4 Capitol

This towering modern hotel boasts the latest in business technologies, as well as a fitness centre and parking. Rooms include dual phone/modem lines, Internet access via your TV, and, in the suites, a private PC, fax, and large screen TV. *Via Cimarosa 6 • 02-438-591 • www.hotelcapitolmilano.com • €€€€*

5 Doria Grand Hotel

A large hotel with modern, comfortable rooms, four conference rooms, and secretarial services. Similar to many hotels in Milan, special discount rates are available on weekends. *Viale Andrea Doria 22 • 02-6741-1411 • www.doriagrandhotel.it • €€€€*

6 Una Hotel Cusani

Formally the Radisson Bonaparte, this hotel is now part of the Una hotel chain. The rooms are spacious and comfortable. A prime location, across from the Castello Sforzesco. *Via Cusani 13 • Map L3 • 02-85-601 • www.unahotels.it • €€€€€*

7 Marriott

With 20 meeting rooms, a well-equipped business centre and a floor of Executive rooms, the Milan Marriott was built for the business traveller. Convenient for the Via Wagner or Piazza De Angeli shopping streets; if only it were nearer the centre for some sightseeing when the meetings are over. *Via Washington 66 • 02-48-521 • www.marriott.com • €€€€*

8 Mediolanum

The austerity of this cement-grey hotel is relieved by the personal touch brought by family management. Facilities include a business centre with secretarial services. *Via Mauro Macchi 1 • 02-670-5312 • www.mediolanumhotel.com • €€€*

9 Atahotel Fieramilano

If you're in town for a trade show, you can get no more convenient a hotel than this, a short walk to the metro for Fieramilano. The hotel's contemporary rooms, over 230 in total, are given a touch of warmth by richly patterned fabrics. *Viale S Boezio 20 • 02-336-221 • www.atahotels.com • €€€€€*

10 Atahotel Executive

This massive hotel on the north end of the Brera district has rooms decorated in sumptuous antique style, skilfully masking its range of high-tech amenities. There's a full-fledged business centre and 21 meeting rooms. *Viale Sturzo 45 • 02-62-941 • www.hotel-executive.com • €€€€€*

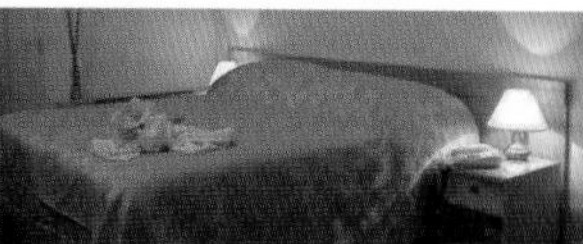

Left **Rovello** Centre **Antica Locanda Solferino** Right **Genius Hotel Downtown**

TOP 10 Milan's Mid-Range Hotels

1 Antica Locanda Solferino

Milan's most eccentric hotel is beloved by fashion gurus and film stars. What it lacks in amenities such as minibars and large bathrooms, it makes up for with its flower-fringed balconies, homely mismatched furnishings and breakfast-in-bed. ✆ *Via Castelfidardo 2 • Map M1 • 02-657-0129 • www.anticalocandasolferino.it • €€€€€*

2 London

The most old-fashioned of three hotels on a block near the Castello offers smiling service, bright, large rooms with worn but solid furnishings, and 10 per cent off the next-door restaurant. Rooms get smaller as you go up each floor, so try for the ground floor. ✆ *Via Rovello 3 • Map L3 • 02-7202-0166 • www.hotellondonmilano.com • €€€*

3 Rovello

In a central location close to Santa Maria delle Grazie, this hotel has shiny wood floors, stylish furnishings, orthopaedic beds and unusually spacious bedrooms. ✆ *Via Rovello 18 • Map L3 • 02-8646-4654 • www.hotel-rovello.it • €€€*

4 Antica Locanda Leonardo

Situated in a residential building just a couple of minutes' walk from Santa Maria delle Grazie and *The Last Supper*, this family-run guesthouse with a small garden offers a peaceful retreat from the bustle of the city. ✆ *Corso Magneta 78 • Map J3 • 02-4801-4197 • www.anticalocandaleonardo.com • €€€€*

5 Ariosto Hotel

Luxurious amenities and refined service without a high price tag. Rooms overlook the private garden or open onto the Liberty-style façades of this residential street, and all come with wood furnishings and high-speed Internet. Free bikes are provided for guests. ✆ *Via Ariosto 22 • 02-481-7844 • www.ariosto.com • €€€*

6 Ariston

A novel approach to Italian inn-keeping: an eco-hotel. The electrical devices are engineered for low power consumption; the showers conserve water; the tap water and even the air are purified; the breakfast spread is organic. Naturally, the desk rents out Riciclo bicycles. ✆ *Largo Carrobbio 2 • Map K/L4 • 02-7200-0556 • www.aristonhotel.com • €€€€*

7 Zurigo

Although the entrance is on a busy street, just 5 minutes' walk from Piazza del Duomo, the compact but well-equipped rooms face the back of the hotel and are very quiet. Riciclo bicycles are available to guests free of charge. ✆ *Corso Italia 11A • Map L/M5 • 02-7202-2260 • www.brerahotels.com • €€€*

8 Genius Hotel Downtown

A cosy modern hotel on a quiet street just beside the Castello with bright, thick carpets, orthopaedic beds and largish baths. There is an entire non-smoking floor. ✆ *Via Porlezza 4 • 02-7209-4644 • www.hotelgenius.it • €€€*

9 Hotel Lancaster

A lovely Art Nouveau-style townhouse in a peaceful residential street right by Parco Sempione, this hotel is within easy reach of the centre of the city. A real find, it offers great prices, especially in June and July. Some rooms have terraces. Closed three weeks in August. ✆ *Via Abbondio Sangiorgio 16 • Map J1 • 02-344-705 • www.hotellancaster.it • €€€€€*

10 Gran Duca di York

In the 19th century this *palazzo* was used by the nearby cathedral to house visiting cardinals. Today, rooms have comfortable, modern furnishings. Some bedrooms have terraces and the location in the historic centre is great. ✆ *Via Moneta 1a • Map L4 • 02-874-863 • www.ducadiyork.com • €€€€*

***Note:** Unless otherwise stated, all hotels on p146 accept credit cards and have en-suite bathrooms and A/C (air conditioning)*

Price Categories

For a standard, double room per night (with breakfast if included), taxes and extra charges.	
€	under €110
€€	€110–€160
€€€	€160–€210
€€€€	€210–€270
€€€€€	over €270

Left **Hotel Sempione** Right **Hotel San Francisco**

TOP 10 Milan's Budget Gems

1 San Francisco

A small family-run hotel only six metro stops from the Duomo and three from the main train station. Rooms are sparse but adequate and there is a pretty little garden with pergola, lawn and paved terrace where breakfast is served in the summer. *Viale Lombardia 55 • Map P1 • 02-236-1009 • www.hotel-sanfrancisco.it • €€*

2 Hotel Sempione

This hotel, located between the train station and Piazza del Duomo, is close to the shopping and entertainment hub of Corso Buenos Aires. The airy and simple rooms offer all modern comforts. *Via Finocchiaro Aprile 11 • Map M5 • 02-6570-323 • www.hotelsempionemilan.com • €*

3 Hotel Due Giardini

Set in a pleasant location, convenient for but not too close to the station, and with the shops in Corso Buenos Aires just a short walk away, this hotel offers great value for money. As its name suggests, it really does have two gardens. *Via Benedetto Marcello 47 • Map P1 • 02-2952-1093 • www.hotelduegiardini.it • €*

4 Paganini

Staying at this tiny hotel on a residential street off Corso Buenos Aires is like moving in with friends. The high-ceilinged rooms are large and kitted out with spare but homely furnishings. Only one of the eight rooms has a private bathroom. *Via Paganini 6 • 02-204-7443 • www.hotelpaganini.it • €*

5 MyHotel Milano

To the west of the city near the Fiera Milano, this pleasant, small hotel located in a converted palace offers impeccable service, great breakfasts and free Wi-Fi. *Via Giasone del Maino 14 • 02-8945-6112 • www.myhotelmilano.it • €*

6 Kennedy

Of the many bare-bones *pensioni* in this neighbourhood near the public gardens and Corso Buenos Aires, the Kennedy singles itself out for cleanliness, friendliness and the fact that its fifth-floor location allows a few rooms to peek over the rooftops at the distant spires of the Duomo. For once, an espresso and croissant in the hotel bar is as cheap as at a local café. *Viale Tunisia 6 • Map P1 • 02-2940-0934 • www.kennedyhotel.it • €*

7 Villa Magnolia

This attractive early-1900s villa in a residential area close to the Navigli district, just south of the city centre, offers bed-and-breakfast accommodation. It has two double rooms and one suite, sleeping three, and has satellite TV. *Via Ambrogio Binda 32 • Map J6 • 02-8130-200 • www.bbvillamagnolia.it • €*

8 Hotel Palladio

A typical 1920s townhouse in a quiet residential street very near the lively Porta Romana area with its many bars, shops and restaurants. This hotel offers excellent value, with special rates June–August. Many rooms have balconies and all have satellite TV. No breakfast served but there's a café several minutes' walk away. *Via Palladio 8 • Map P6 • 02-5830-6900 • www.hotelpalladio.eu • €*

9 Vecchia Milano

It's on the high end of inexpensive, but worth it for the charming, semi-rustic wood panelling, good-sized rooms and location on a quiet street west of the Duomo. Some of the rooms come with third beds that flip down from the wall – great for budget-minded families. *Via Borromei 4 • Map L4 • 02-875-042 • www.hotel vecchiamilano.it • €*

10 Ostello Piero Rotta

Milan's rather institutional hostel is located outside the city centre, near the San Siro stadium and Fieramilanocity. It has a pretty garden. *Via M Bassi 2 • 02-3926-7095 • www.hostelmilan.org • €*

Left **Agnello d'Oro, Bergamo** Centre **Broletto, Mantua** Right **I Due Roccoli, Iseo**

TOP 10 Hotels in the Smaller Towns

1 San Lorenzo, Bergamo

The classiest hotel in Bergamo opened in 1998 at the north end of the atmospheric upper town. The service is impeccable, and the 30 rooms have pleasing minimalist decor. *Piazza Mascheroni 9a • Map D3 • 035-237-383 • www.hotelsanlorenzobg.it • €€*

2 Agnello d'Oro, Bergamo

Built in 1600, the hotel has a mountain chalet look to it. The receptionists can be brusque, but the rooms are cosy, if unimaginatively furnished. Book a room at the front, where small, flower-filled balconies give views over the bustling main drag below. *Via Gombito 22 • Map D3 • 035-249-883 • www.agnellodoro.it €*

3 Hotel Casa Poli, Mantua

A boutique hotel with original Art Nouveau façade, just a 15-minute walk from the city centre. All 34 rooms are decorated in their own individual style. A pretty inner courtyard offers a perfect place for pre-dinner drinks. *Corso Garibaldi 32 • Map H6 • 0376-288-170 www.hotelcasapoli.it • €€€*

4 Broletto, Mantua

Small, family-run hotel in a 16th-century *palazzo* with a vaguely rustic contemporary decor. Just metres from Lake Inferiore. *Via Accademia 1 • Map H6 • 0376-326-784 • www.hotelbroletto.com • €€*

5 Hotel Impero, Cremona

The 53 rooms of this hotel are elegantly decorated, combining period furniture and modern facilities. Located in the town centre, the hotel offers views over the cathedral square and the town hall. *Piazza della Pace 21 • Map E6 • 0372-413-013 • www.cremonahotels.it • €*

6 I Due Roccoli, Iseo

Set in its own quiet park high above the lake on the road to Polaveno, this family-run hotel offers a countryside escape of rustic-tinged rooms and splendid views of the lake and mountains. There is a tennis court, a pool and an excellent restaurant *(see p129). Via Silvio Bonomelli • Map E4 • 030-982-2977 • www.idueroccoli.com • Closed Nov–Mar • €€*

7 Iseolago, Iseo

The Iseolago is situated near the Torbiere nature reserve and mixes the best of a resort hotel with the class of a fine inn. There is a fitness centre, two pools, tennis courts, and watersports at the beach. The one drawback is that it is in the suburbs, so you need a car. *Via Colombera 2 • Map E4 • 030-98-891 • www.iseolagohotel.it • €€*

8 Villa Crespi, Lake Orta

This fantastical 1879 Moorish-style villa, complete with minaret, is set against a backdrop of mountains. Suites and rooms are sumptuous, with mosaic or parquet flooring, carved wooden furnishings, silk brocaded walls, and bed canopies. The Michelin-starred restaurant is excellent *(see p129). Via Fava, 18 • Map A3 • 0322-911-902 • www.villacrespi.it • Closed Jan–Feb • €€€€*

9 Villa Principe Leopoldo, Lake Lugano

This bastion of 19th-century luxury overlooks Lugano from its Swiss hillside. Facilities range from a business centre to a fitness room, beauty spa and swimming pool. The Villa offers sumptuous suites; the Residence annex more subdued double rooms. *Via Montalbano 5 • Map B1 • 0041-919-858-855 • www.leopoldohotel.com • €€€€€*

10 Vittoria, Brescia

Located in the very centre, this hotel offers all the five-star amenities you could ask for in an imposing Fascist-era pile. Freestanding columns in two of the five suites are a nice touch. Rooms on the fourth floor offer views of the castle. *Via X Giornate 20 • Map F4 • 030-280-061 • www.hotelvittoria.com • €€€€*

For hotels around the main Lakes **see pp103, 113 and 123**
For an explanation of price symbols **see p147**

Left **Camping sign** Centre **Brione camp site** Right **The pool at Campeggio Garda Giulia**

TOP 10 Self-Catering and Camp Sites

1 Residence Aramis Milano, Milan

Overlooking a canal in the lively Navigli district, this "aparthotel" has accommodation ranging from rooms to fully equipped apartments sleeping six. All clean and spacious, and with free Wi-Fi. *Via Mortaro 2 • Map J6 • 0340-084-8590 • www.residencearamismilano.it • €–€€€*

2 Residence di Corso Italia, Milan

These apartments are near the city centre and public transport. Decor is smart and modern and some rooms have a terrace. Children's cots, laundry and parking are available for a small fee, and there's a coffee bar on the premises. *Corso Italia 34 • Map L5 • 02-72-4311 • www.residencedicorsoitalia.it • €€*

3 Milanosuites, Milan

A sister operation of, and located next to, the Antica Locanda dei Mercanti *(see p144)*, these five suites have one or two bedrooms with en-suite bathroom and living room. Special rates for weekly rentals. *Via San Tomaso 6 • Map L3 • 02-8051-023 • www.milanosuites.it • €€€€€*

4 Camping Isolino, Verbania, Lake Maggiore

This oasis of tranquility sits on the promontory of a natural reserve along a private sandy beach. It's one of the best-equipped in the region, with a market, pizzeria, restaurant, video games, pool, mountain bike excursions, windsurfing lessons and entertainment. *Via per Feriolo 25 • Map A2 • 0323-496-414 • www.campinisolino.com • Closed Oct–Mar • €*

5 Camping Conca d'Oro, Feriolo di Baveno, Lake Maggiore

This verdant campground lies outside Baveno in the Fondo Toce nature reserve. Amenities include a restaurant, mini-market, bikes and kayaks, video games and a sandy beach. *Via 42 Martiri 26 • Map A2 • 0323-281-16 • www.concadoro.it • Closed Oct–Mar • €*

6 Camping Villaggio Gefara, Domaso, Lake Como

This small campground sits right on the beach, with a bar and laundry room, beach volleyball, and plenty of shops and watersports nearby. *Via Case Sparse 230 • Map C2 • 0344-96-163 • www.campinggefara.it • Closed 6 Oct–20 Mar • €*

7 Camping Monte Brione, Riva, Lake Garda

Set in greenery near the beach, the camping and caravan site has minigolf, swimming and table tennis. Small tents can be pitched amid olive terraces. *Riva del Garda, Via Brione 32 • Map H3 • 0464-520-885 • www.campingbrione.com • Closed Oct–Mar • €*

8 Campeggio Garda Giulia, Limone, Lake Garda

Just outside the centre of Limone, on its own private beach, this camping site offers windsurfing and sailing, and two pools, as well as a fish restaurant, wood-oven pizzeria, beach grill, and supermarket. *Via 4 Novembre 10 • Map G3 • 0365-954-550 • www.campinglagodigarda.it • Closed Nov–Mar • €*

9 Camping del Sole, Lake Iseo

This large camping site offers plenty of greenery right on the lake (book ahead for the precious few lakeside sites). Facilities include a restaurant, market, cycle hire, laundry, as well as two pools and tennis and basketball courts. *Via per Rovato 26 • Map E4 • 030-980-288 • www.campingdelsole.it • Closed Oct–Mar • €*

10 Campeggio Città di Milano

Milan's only campground is by the SS22 road to Novara (take bus 72 from the De Angeli Metro stop) near the San Siro stadium. It has a restaurant and there is a waterpark nearby. *Via G Airaghi 61 • 02-4820-7017 • www.campingmilano.it • €*

Depending on size, amenities, location and style, apartments can range from €500 to €2,500 per week

General Index

Index

Page numbers in **bold** type refer to main entries.

Acknowledgments

The Author
Reid Bramblett is a travel writer who currently lives in New York. He has written guides to Italy, Europe and New York for Frommer's and is the author of DK's *Top 10 Tuscany.*

Additional Contributions
Roberta Kedzierski

Produced by
BLUE ISLAND PUBLISHING, London
www.blueisland.co.uk

Editorial Director
Rosalyn Thiro

Art Director
Stephen Bere

Associate Editor
Michael Ellis

Editors
Charlotte Rundall, Jane Simmonds

Designer
Lee Redmond

Picture Research
Ellen Root

Research Assistance
Amaia Allende

Proofreader
Jane Simmonds

Fact-checker
Sylvia Gallotti

Indexer
Charlotte Rundall

Main Photographers
Paul Harris and Anne Heslope

Additional Photography
Steve Bere, John Heseltine, Clive Streeter

Cartography
James Anderson, Jane Voss (Anderson Geographics Ltd)

AT DORLING KINDERSLEY

Publisher
Douglas Amrine

Publishing Manager
Anna Streiffert

Senior Art Editor
Marisa Renzullo

Senior Cartographic Editor
Casper Morris

Senior DTP Designer
Jason Little

Production
Melanie Dowland

Revisions Team
Marta Bescos, Sally-Ann Bloomfield, Michelle Crane, Cristina Dainotto, Julie Dunn, Nicola Erdpresser, Fay Franklin, Amy Harrison, Roberta Kedzierski, Nicola Malone, Alison McGill, Catherine Palmi, Quadrum Solutions Pvt Ltd, Rada Radojicic, Sands Publishing Solutions, Ellie Smith, Julie Thompson, Conrad Van Dyk

Photography Permissions
Dorling Kindersley would like to thank all the cathedrals, churches, museums, hotels, restaurants, bars, clubs, shops, galleries and other sights for their assistance and kind permission to photograph.

Key: a-above; b-below/bottom; c-centre; f-far; l-left; r-right; t-top.

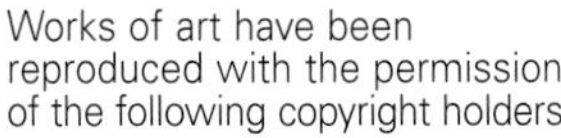

Works of art have been reproduced with the permission of the following copyright holders:

ALAMY IMAGES: MAF 128tr; Rolf Richardson 124tc; ANTICA LOCANDA SOLFERINO: 146tc; ARCHIVIO ISTITUTO GEOGRAFICO DEAGOSTINI: 24br, 24bl; ARCHIVIO STORICO DEL CINEMA/ AFE: directed by Mario Camerini 50tl, directed by Michelangelo Antonioni 50tr, directed by Charles Vidor 50c, directed by Vittorio De Sica 50b.

BRIDGEMAN ART LIBRARY, London: Biblioteca Ambrosiana, Milan 48tc; Ognissanti, Florence Sandro Botticelli Detail from *St Augustine in his Study* 33tr; Museo del Duomo Tintoretto *Christ Among the Doctors* 73b; Pinacoteca Ambrosiana 7tl, 18c, 18-19; Pinacoteca di Brera 13c, 14cl, 15b, 48b; Sandro Botticelli *Portrait of Guiliano de' Medici* 27b; Private Collection 32tr, 33cr.

CLAUDIO AMADEI PHOTOGRAPHER: 68tl; COLLEONI & DELL' ANGELO: 129tl; CORBIS: Ted Spiegel 46tr; Sandro Vannini 47t.

DISCOTECA ALCATRAZ: 60tr.

GENIUS RESORT: 146tr.

HOTEL PIRONI: 103tl; HOTEL SAN FRANCISCO: 147tc; HOTEL SEMPIONE 147tl.

LEONARDO MEDIA LTD.: 81tc.

MAGAZZINI GENERALI: 61t; T Conti 6bl, 12c, 14t, 40tl, 52tr; M Cristofori 40b; C Dogliani 40tc; D Donadoni 7tr, 24–5 27t, 60b; G Ferrari 52c; F Garufi 33br; S Malli 8t, 24t, 88tr; G Mereghetti 52tl; Foto OM 53tr; F Pizzochero 66tr, 67tl.

PEC SPA: 79tr; PICTURES COLOUR LIBRARY: Picture Finders 78tr.

RISTORANTE CAVALLINO: 122tl; ROVELLO HOTEL:146tl.

SANTA MARTA HOTEL: 146tc; © PHOTO SCALA, Florence: Biblioteca Marucelliana, Firenze Leoni Ottavio 48tr; Biblioteca Reale, Torino 48c; Castello Sforzesco 16t, 16b, 16–17, 17t, 17b; Galleria degli Uffizi - courtesy of the Ministero Beni e Att. Culturali 32bl; Museo Poldi-Pezzoli 41b, 75b; Museo Teatrale alla Scala © DACS 2011 41t; Palazzo Ducale Venezia Federico Zuccari *Il Barbarossa bacia il piede a papa Alessandro III* 32tl; Pinacoteca Ambrosiana 18b, 19c, 19b; Pinacoteca di Brera 12t, 12b, 12–13, 13b, 14b, 15t, 48tl; Sant'Ambrogio 20t, 20bl, 20br, 21t, 21c, 20–21, 21b; Santa Maria delle Grazie 6tl, 8c(d), 8b(d), 9t(d), 8–9, 9b(d), 30–1.

TEATRO ALLA SCALA: 53bl; Il Marchesino 65br.

UFFICIO STAMPA ORCHESTRA VERDI: Silvia Lelli 60tl.

Phrase Book

n an Emergency

lelp!	**Aiuto!**	eye-yoo-toh
top!	**Fermo!**	fair-moh
all a doctor.	**Chiama un medico**	kee-ah-mah oon meh-dee-koh
all an ambulance.	**Chiama un' ambulanza**	kee-ah-mah oon am-boo-lan-tsa
all the police.	**Chiama la polizia**	kee-ah-mah lah pol-ee-tsee-ah
all the fire brigade.	**Chiama i pompieri**	kee-ah-mah ee pom-pee-air-ee

ommunication Essentials

es/No	**Si/No**	see/noh
lease	**Per favore**	pair fah-vor-eh
hank you	**Grazie**	grah-tsee-eh
xcuse me	**Mi scusi**	mee skoo-zee
lello	**Buon giorno**	bwon jor-noh
oodbye	**Arrivederci**	ah-ree-veh-dair-chee
ood evening	**Buona sera**	bwon-ah sair-ah
/hat?	**Quale?**	kwah-leh?
/hen?	**Quando?**	kwan-doh?
/hy?	**Perchè?**	pair-keh?
/here?	**Dove?**	doh-veh?

seful Phrases

low are you?	**Come sta?**	koh-meh stah?
ery well, hank you.	**Molto bene, grazie.**	moll-toh beh-neh grah-tsee-eh
leased to meet you.	**Piacere di conoscerla.**	pee-ah-chair-eh dee-coh-noh-shair-lah
hat's fine.	**Va bene.**	va beh-neh
/here is/are ...?	**Dov'è/ Dove sono ...?**	dov-eh/doveh soh-noh?
ow do get to ...?	**Come faccio per arrivare a ...?**	koh-meh fah-choh pair arri-var-eh ah...?
o you speak English?	**Parla inglese?**	par-lah een-gleh-zeh?
don't nderstand.	**Non capisco.**	non ka-pee-skoh
m sorry.	**Mi dispiace.**	mee dee-spee-ah-cheh

hopping

low much loes this cost?	**Quant'è, per favore?**	kwan-the pair fah-vor-eh?
would like ...	**Vorrei ...**	vor-ray
o you have ...?	**Avete ...?**	ah-veh-teh... ?
o you take redit cards?	**Accettate carte di credito?**	ah-chet-tah-the kar-teh dee creh-dee-toh?
/hat time do ou open/close?	**A che ora apre/ chiude?**	ah keh or-ah ah-preh/ kee-oo-deh?
is one	**questo**	kweh-stoh
at one	**quello**	kwell-oh
xpensive	**caro**	kar-oh
heap	**a buon prezzo**	ah bwon pret-soh
ze, clothes	**la taglia**	lah tah-lee-ah
ze, shoes	**il numero**	eel noo-mair-oh
/hite	**bianco**	bee-ang-koh
lack	**nero**	neh-roh
ed	**rosso**	ross-oh
ellow	**giallo**	jal-loh
reen	**verde**	vair-deh
ue	**blu**	bloo

Types of Shop

bakery	**il forno /il panificio**	eel forn-oh /il /eel pan-ee-fee-choh
bank	**la banca**	lah bang-kah
bookshop	**la libreria**	lah lee-breh-ree-ah
cake shop	**la pasticceria**	lah pas-tee-chair-ee-ah
chemist	**la farmacia**	lah far-mah-chee-ah
delicatessen	**la salumeria**	lah sah-loo-meh-ree-ah
department store	**il grande magazzino**	eel gran-deh mag-gad-zee-noh
grocery	**alimentari**	ah-lee-men-tah-ree
hairdresser	**il parrucchiere**	eel par-oo-kee-air-eh
ice cream parlour	**la gelateria**	lah jel-lah-tair-ree-ah
market	**il mercato**	eel mair-kah-toh
newsstand	**l'edicola**	leh-dee-koh-lah
post office	**l'ufficio postale**	loo-fee-choh pos-tah-leh
supermarket	**il supermercato**	eel su-pair-mair-kah-toh
tobacconist	**il tabaccaio**	eel tah-bak-eye-oh
travel agency	**l'agenzia di viaggi**	lah-jen-tsee-ah dee vee-ad-jee

Sightseeing

art gallery	**la pinacoteca**	lah peena-koh-teh-kah
bus stop	**la fermata dell'autobus**	lah fair-mah-tah dell ow-toh-booss
church	**la chiesa la basilica**	lah kee-eh-zah la lah bah-seel-i-kah
closed for holidays	**chiuso per le ferie**	kee-oo-zoh pair leh fair-ee-eh
garden	**il giardino**	eel jar-dee-no
museum	**il museo**	eel moo-zeh-oh
railway station	**la stazione**	lah stah-tsee-oh-neh
tourist information	**l'ufficio di turismo**	loo-fee-choh dee too-ree-smoh

Staying in a Hotel

Do you have any vacant rooms?	**Avete camere libere?**	ah-veh-teh kah-mair-eh lee-bair-eh?
double room	**una camera doppia**	oona kah-mair-ah doh-pee-ah
with double bed	**con letto matrimoniale**	kon let-toh-mah tree-moh-nee-ah-leh
twin room	**una camera con due letti**	oona kah-mair-ah kon doo-eh let-tee?
single room	**una camera singola**	oona kah-mair-ah sing-goh-lah
room with a bath, shower	**una camera con bagno, con doccia**	oona kah-mair-ah kon ban-yoh, kon dot-chah
I have a reservation.	**Ho fatto una prenotazione.**	oh fat-toh oona preh-noh-tah-tsee-oh-neh

Eating Out

Have you got a table for ...?	**Avete un tavolo per ... ?**	ah-veh-teh oon tah-voh-loh pair ...?
I'd like to reserve a table	**Vorrei riservare un tavolo**	vor-ray ree-sair-vah-reh oon tah-voh-loh
breakfast	**colazione**	koh-lah-tsee-oh-neh
lunch	**pranzo**	pran-tsoh
dinner	**cena**	cheh-nah
The bill, please.	**Il conto, per favore.**	eel kon-toh pair fah-vor-eh
waitress	**cameriera**	kah-mair-ee-air-ah
waiter	**cameriere**	kah-mair-ee-air-eh
fixed price menu	**il menù a prezzo fisso**	eel meh-noo ah pret-soh fee-soh
dish of the day	**piatto del giorno**	pee-ah-toh dell jor-no
starter	**antipasto**	an-tee-pass-toh
first course	**il primo**	eel pree-moh
main course	**il secondo**	eel seh-kon-doh
vegetables	**contorni**	eel kon-tor-noh
dessert	**il dolce**	eel doll-cheh
cover charge	**il coperto**	eel koh-pair-toh
wine list	**la lista dei vini**	lah lee-stah day vee-nee
glass	**il bicchiere**	eel bee-kee-air-eh
bottle	**la bottiglia**	lah bot-teel-yah
knife	**il coltello**	eel kol-tell-oh
fork	**la forchetta**	lah for-ket-tah
spoon	**il cucchiaio**	eel koo-kee-eye-oh

Menu Decoder

l'acqua minerale gassata/ naturale	lah-kwah mee-nair-ah-leh gah-zah-tah/ nah-too-rah-leh	mineral water fizzy/still
agnello	ah-niell-oh	lamb
aglio	al-ee-oh	garlic
al forno	al for-noh	baked
alla griglia	ah-lah greel-yah	grilled
arrosto	ar-ross-toh	roast
la birra	lah beer-rah	beer
la bistecca	lah bee-stek-kah	steak
il burro	eel boor-oh	butter
il caffè	eel kah-feh	coffee
la carne	la kar-neh	meat
carne di maiale	kar-neh dee mah-yah-leh	pork
la cipolla	la chip-oh-lah	onion
i fagioli	ee fah-joh-lee	beans
il formaggio	eel for-mad-joh	cheese
le fragole	leh frah-goh-leh	strawberries
il fritto misto	eel free-toh mees-toh	mixed fried dish
la frutta	la froot-tah	fruit
frutti di mare	froo-tee dee mah-reh	seafood
i funghi	ee foon-ghee	mushrooms
i gamberi	ee gam-bair-ee	prawns
il gelato	eel jel-lah-toh	ice cream
l'insalata	leen-sah-lah-tah	salad
il latte	eel laht-teh	milk
lesso	less-oh	boiled
il manzo	eel man-tsoh	beef
l'olio	loh-lee-oh	oil
il pane	eel pah-neh	bread
le patate	leh pah-tah-teh	potatoes
le patatine fritte	leh pah-tah-teen-eh free-teh	chips
il pepe	eel peh-peh	pepper
il pesce	eel pesh-eh	fish
il pollo	eel poll-oh	chicken
il pomodoro	eel poh-moh-dor-oh	tomato
il prosciutto cotto/crudo	eel pro-shoo-toh kot-toh/kroo-doh	ham cooked/cured
il riso	eel ree-zoh	rice
il sale	eel sah-leh	salt
la salsiccia	lah sal-see-chah	sausage
succo d'arancia/ di limone	soo-koh dah-ran-chah/ dee lee-moh-neh	orange/lemon juice
il tè	eel teh	tea
la torta	lah tor-tah	cake/tart
l'uovo	loo-oh-voh	egg
vino bianco	vee-noh bee-ang-koh	white wine
vino rosso	vee-noh ross-oh	red wine
il vitello	eel vee-tell-oh	veal
le vongole	leh von-goh-leh	clams
lo zucchero	loh zoo-kair-oh	sugar
la zuppa	lah tsoo-pah	soup

Numbers

1	**uno**	oo-noh
2	**due**	doo-eh
3	**tre**	treh
4	**quattro**	kwat-roh
5	**cinque**	ching-kweh
6	**sei**	say-ee
7	**sette**	set-teh
8	**otto**	ot-toh
9	**nove**	noh-veh
10	**dieci**	dee-eh-chee
11	**undici**	oon-dee-chee
12	**dodici**	doh-dee-chee
13	**tredici**	tray-dee-chee
14	**quattordici**	kwat-tor-dee-chee
15	**quindici**	kwin-dee-chee
16	**sedici**	say-dee-chee
17	**diciassette**	dee-chah-set-the
18	**diciotto**	dee-chot-toh
19	**diciannove**	dee-chah-noh-veh
20	**venti**	ven-tee
30	**trenta**	tren-tah
40	**quaranta**	kwah-ran-tah
50	**cinquanta**	ching-kwan-tah
60	**sessanta**	sess-an-tah
70	**settanta**	set-tan-tah
80	**ottanta**	ot-tan-tah
90	**novanta**	noh-van-tah
100	**cento**	chen-toh
1,000	**mille**	mee-leh
2,000	**duemila**	doo-eh mee-lah
1,000,000	**un milione**	oon meel-yoh-neh

Time

one minute	**un minuto**	oon mee-noo-toh
one hour	**un'ora**	oon or-ah
a day	**un giorno**	oon jor-noh
Monday	**lunedì**	loo-neh-dee
Tuesday	**martedì**	mar-teh-dee
Wednesday	**mercoledì**	mair-koh-leh-dee
Thursday	**giovedì**	joh-veh-dee
Friday	**venerdì**	ven-air-dee
Saturday	**sabato**	sah-bah-toh
Sunday	**domenica**	doh-meh-nee-ka